"Biblical theology is the essential starting place for understanding Scripture rightly. This short, accessible book will help you grasp the Bible's big story by tracing the most important themes of Scripture from Genesis to Revelation. This is a tremendous resource for pastors and congregations alike. Let Chris Bruno give you a guided tour of the central themes of Scripture—you won't regret it."

R. Albert Mohler Jr., President and Joseph Emerson Brown
Professor of Christian Theology, The Southern Baptist Theological
Seminary

"Here is an ideal resource for either personal Bible study or for small-group curriculum. Chris Bruno's concise and readable explanation of sixteen biblical words or concepts provides a lens through which we can see the overall message of the Bible with greater precision. Readers of this book will be better equipped to grasp how the parts of the Bible relate to the whole and how all of history can be understood through biblical theology."

Chris Brauns, Pastor, The Red Brick Church, Stillman Valley,
Illinois; author, *Unpacking Forgiveness, Bound Together,* and *When the Word Leads Your Pastoral Search*

"Chris offers a clear, brief, and winsome trip through the pages of Scripture as he examines major unifying themes of the narrative of redemption. This is a wonderful contribution to the growing number of works that help Christians learn biblical theology; it helps us 'put our Bibles together' and better grasp the story of God's saving reign through Jesus. I commend this book to you, and pray that it blesses and teaches many in the church."

Jon Nielson, Ministry Director, Christian Union, Princeton
University; coeditor, *Gospel-Centered Youth Ministry*

"Trustworthy tools like this are greatly needed for equipping the saints to understand and apply the whole story of the Bible to all of life and ministry. I'm looking forward to putting this resource to work."

Bill Walsh, Director of International Outreach, The Gospel
Coalition

T0317385

"Building on the success of his incredibly helpful work *The Whole Story of the Bible in 16 Verses*, Chris Bruno returns to his craft to produce an equally powerful tool for the church in her mission to make disciples. Bruno displays his insightful grasp of biblical theology and his passion for developing the next generation of servant-disciples in a style that is both accessible to the average layperson and challenging even to the most seasoned believer. Allowing his personality to shine through on each page, Bruno guides his readers through a full-orbed understanding of God's story through the entirety of the Bible. Brilliant in its structure and its delivery, *The Whole Message of the Bible in 16 Words* promises to live up to the high standard Bruno has already set and, more importantly, serve the global church in her understanding of God's Word."

Jonathan Arnold, Assistant Professor of Christian Theology and Church History and Director of The Augustine Honors Collegium, Boyce College; Fellow, Andrew Fuller Center for Baptist Studies

"The Great Commission is a thread that weaves its way through the gospel story from beginning to end. Chris simply and clearly brings out the themes of God's Word that form the basis for Christian life and mission. *The Whole Message of the Bible in 16 Words* takes serious biblical theology and makes it accessible and enjoyable. This book will be a blessing to the church in America and around the world."

Scott Dunford, Vice President of Mobilization, ABWE International

*The Whole Message of
the Bible in 16 Words*

THE WHOLE MESSAGE
OF THE BIBLE IN
16 WORDS

Chris Bruno

WHEATON, ILLINOIS

The Whole Message of the Bible in 16 Words

Copyright © 2017 by Christopher R. Bruno

Published by Crossway
          1300 Crescent Street
          Wheaton, Illinois 60187

All rights reserved. No part of this publication may be reproduced, stored in a retrieval system, or transmitted in any form by any means, electronic, mechanical, photocopy, recording, or otherwise, without the prior permission of the publisher, except as provided for by USA copyright law. Crossway® is a registered trademark in the United States of America.

Cover design: Brian Bobel

First printing 2017

Printed in the United States of America

Unless otherwise indicated, all Scripture quotations are from the ESV® Bible (The Holy Bible, English Standard Version®), copyright © 2001 by Crossway, a publishing ministry of Good News Publishers. Used by permission. All rights reserved.

Scripture quotations marked MESSAGE are from *The Message*. Copyright © by Eugene H. Peterson 1993, 1994, 1995, 1996, 2000, 2001, 2002. Used by permission of NavPress Publishing Group.

Scripture references marked NIV are taken from The Holy Bible, New International Version®, NIV®. Copyright © 1973, 1978, 1984, 2011 by Biblica, Inc.™ Used by permission. All rights reserved worldwide.

All emphases in Scripture quotations have been added by the author.

Trade paperback ISBN: 978-1-4335-5362-2
ePub ISBN: 978-1-4335-5365-3
PDF ISBN: 978-1-4335-5363-9
Mobipocket ISBN: 978-1-4335-5364-6

Library of Congress Cataloging-in-Publication Data

Names: Bruno, Chris, 1980- author.
Title: The whole message of the Bible in 16 words / Chris Bruno.
Description: Wheaton : Crossway, 2017. | Includes bibliographical references and index.
Identifiers: LCCN 2016008968 (print) | LCCN 2016037649 (ebook) | ISBN 9781433553622 (tp) |
    ISBN 9781433553653 (epub) | ISBN 9781433553639 (pdf) | ISBN 9781433553646 (mobi)
Subjects: LCSH: Bible—Theology.
Classification: LCC BS543 .B684 2017 (print) | LCC BS543 (ebook) | DDC 230/.041—dc23
LC record available at https://lccn.loc.gov/2016008968

Crossway is a publishing ministry of Good News Publishers.

VP   25   24   23   22   21   20   19   18   17
14   13   12   11   10   9   8   7   6   5   4   3   2   1

To my parents,
Jerry and Kim Bruno,
who have constantly pointed me to the
God who makes all things new

CONTENTS

PREFACE

The book you are holding is a sequel of sorts to my earlier book *The Whole Story of the Bible in 16 Verses*. In that book, I wanted readers to understand the importance of seeing the whole Bible as one big story, so I picked sixteen key passages as stopping points, or prominent trees, in the big-picture forest of the Bible. While you don't have to read that book before you read this one, this book might be more useful if you have a handle on the story of the Bible. If you want a short, accessible introduction to the storyline of Scripture, *The Whole Story of the Bible in 16 Verses* might help.

In the preface to that book, I say that it is important to see both the forest and the trees of the biblical story. In this book, I want to change our analogy. Instead of talking about the forest and the trees, I want us to see the whole story of the Bible as a rope that is woven tightly together. The goal of this book is to pull out sixteen key strands that compose this rope, look at how they contribute to the overall message, and then put them back in place.

Another image we can use for the structure of this book is a building. In the first two chapters, we are going to lay a foundation by thinking about God and his plan in history—in reverse order. Then we will look at three themes that frame the structure of the overall message of the Bible: creation, covenant, and kingdom. The third and longest section will cover eleven other themes. We can think of these as the superstructure of our building.

I'll go ahead and warn you that at times we'll have to paint with some fairly broad strokes. So I've suggested two "connecting verses" at the end of each chapter—one from the Old Testament and one from the New Testament. Take a few minutes at the end of every chapter to read each verse in its larger context and to reflect on how each one connects with the other verse, with the theme of that chapter, and with the whole message of the Bible. I've also provided a short summary statement at the end of each chapter to help you remember the main points.

At the beginning of my previous book, I say that if you are reading that book, you are interested in biblical theology, even if you don't know it yet. The same is true for this follow-up. The goal of biblical theology is to trace the progressive development of a theme or cluster of themes in the Bible. In this book, we are going to trace sixteen words that help us better understand and apply the whole message of the Bible. If you are reading this book, then, you are on your way to becoming a biblical theologian!

ACKNOWLEDGMENTS

Anyone who thinks that writing isn't a team sport probably hasn't written very much. More people than I could mention in this brief section have helped me with this book.

My wife, Katie, read the entire manuscript and helped to improve the original product in many ways. She and my sons, Luke, Simon, Elliot, and Noah, unfailingly support me and always remind me of what matters most. They also provide me with some great illustrations, and they all at least feign excitement about their dad's books.

As I developed the material and basic structure of the book, Jared Compton, Matt Dirks, David Griffiths, Kevin McFadden, Todd Morikawa, Christian Siania, and Justin White all gave valuable input that shaped the project. The fellows of the Center for Pastor Theologians helped me refine and rework the structure of the book. David Griffiths read an earlier draft of the whole manuscript and helped strengthen it in several ways. I'm eager to return the favor when he starts writing more.

During the early stages of the writing of this book, I served at Northland International University. The entire staff, especially the administrative team I worked with there—Daniel Patz, Scott Dunford, and Jonathan Arnold—was beyond encouraging as

I pursued this and other projects. While writing most of the manuscript, I served at Cedarville University, where the president, Thomas White, and my dean, Jason Lee, along with the rest of my colleagues in the Bible department, provided support and good interaction along the way. Special thanks are due Ched Spellman, who read the entire manuscript and provided valuable feedback as well.

Besides using it in my courses at both Northland and Cedarville, I presented some of this material at Brantwood Baptist Church in Dayton, Ohio; Addison Street Community Church in Chicago, Illinois; and the Grace Partners Fellowship in greater Milwaukee, Wisconsin. I'm grateful to these groups for helping to refine my thinking in several ways.

I also have to thank the team at Crossway for their help—in particular Dave DeWit, who has become a valuable mentor to this young author, and Greg Bailey, who vastly improved the quality of the manuscript.

If I tried to list all the people who have prayed for me as I've worked on this book, I might exceed my word limit and fall out of the good graces of those nice Crossway people I just thanked. You know who you are. Your prayers have been crucial. I'm more grateful than you know.

Finally, this book is dedicated to my parents, Jerry and Kim Bruno. It has not been an easy year for them, but I have seen the way the whole message of the Bible shapes the way they respond to hardship, and I'm grateful to have examples like them. Thank you, Mom and Dad, for pointing me to the God who makes all things new. To him alone be glory.

PART 1

THE
FOUNDATION

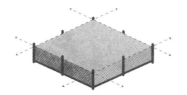

1

THE END

We begin at the end, because the end actually starts in the beginning. Confused? Just hang with me for a little while, and hopefully you'll see where we are heading.

If you knew in advance that Frodo survives the journey to Mordor in *The Lord of the Rings*, but only barely; that Darth Vader is Luke Skywalker's dad in *Star Wars*; and that Bruce Willis is dead the whole time in the *Sixth Sense*, would it ruin these stories? You might think that it would, but according to a 2011 study published in *Psychological Science*, people actually enjoy stories more when they know the ending.[1] What we call "spoilers" could actually be called "improvers"!

Whether that study is right or not, knowing the end of the story of the Bible not only increases our enjoyment of it, but is also crucial for understanding it.

Making All Things New

In one of the last chapters in our Bibles, the apostle John describes the incomprehensible vision that God gave him of the end of history:

> And I heard a loud voice from the throne saying, "Behold, the dwelling place of God is with man. He will dwell with them, and they will be his people, and God himself will be with them as their God. He will wipe away every tear from their eyes, and death shall be no more, neither shall there be mourning, nor crying, nor pain anymore, for the former things have passed away."
>
> And he who was seated on the throne said, "Behold, I am making all things new." Also he said, "Write this down, for these words are trustworthy and true." (Rev. 21:3–5)

These words, God tells us, are trustworthy and true. They are the reality we need to cling to in the midst of a confusing world. Because our lives are filled with summer blockbusters, increasingly amazing technological advances, and so many comfortable things, it can often be easy to forget what is *really real*. But the hope and reality of every Christian is that God himself—not the president, Parliament, or the United Nations—is making all things new. This reality should change the way we see everything in the world—and the way we read everything in our Bibles. We need to see that the end of the Bible is closely connected to the beginning of the story. But we also need to see that the end of the story changes the way we live right now, because the end has already been brought into the present.

Even if you have not read Genesis recently, you probably know the main idea of the creation story. God made the world and everything in it. He created humans in his own image and put them in the garden of Eden. But Adam and Eve doubted God's kindness to them and wanted to be like him, so they ate the fruit from the tree of the knowledge of good and evil (the *only* fruit they weren't allowed to eat). Because of their disobedience, the world and everything in it was broken. And that is basically what we see when we look out the window or turn on the news today. We live in a world where we can still see God's hand in both the beauty of creation and the creativity of people, but it is also a world filled with broken people looking for some way to fix everything that has gone wrong.

If we really want to understand the story of the world and the story of the Bible, we need to see that God told us about the solution almost as soon as we broke the world. And he started to provide for that solution as soon as he told us about it. In Genesis 3:15, he told Adam and Eve that the seed of the woman would crush the head of the Serpent. In other words, he would undo the fall and restore his good creation. From the very beginning, God was committed to stepping into history to change it, renew it, and make it better than we could ever imagine—for our good and his glory. And that, in a nutshell, is what we mean by eschatology.

When many Christians talk about eschatology, they are thinking about a way to understand biblical prophecy and such events as the rapture, the return of Jesus, and the millennium. More often than not, they have charts and timelines to help graph all of these events, and many of them are more than happy to guess where we are on those timelines and how close we might be to the end of the world. The word *eschatology* literally means "the study of the last things," so you can understand why the emphasis is on these sorts of questions.

The return of Christ and the new creation is obviously a big part of what we mean by eschatology. But I have something bigger in mind. When I talk about eschatology, it starts with God keeping his promises, forgiving sin, sending his Spirit, and reigning as King.

So when we talk about the end, we can't just start with the

last page of the Bible. We need to see everything that God has done and is doing to get us to that last page. While we need to see that eschatology is heading toward the end, we also need to see that the end shapes the whole story. In fact, that is how I would define eschatology—the study of God's work in history to bring the story to his intended end. So when we talk eschatology, we have to start in Genesis.

Eschatology in the Old Testament

Just after Adam and Eve sinned in the garden, God promised that Eve's offspring would crush the head of the Serpent. In other words, he promised that, through the line of Adam and Eve, he would defeat the Serpent and reverse the fall. Adam and Eve were designed to be God's representative rulers in the garden—that is a big part of what it means to be made in his image. But they failed to rule as God intended. And because of this, both the human race and creation itself no longer reflect God's perfect rule over them. We call this the curse.

So a big part of God's work in history is reestablishing his perfect reign as King over all things. Throughout the Old Testament, we see God working to do just that—first through his people Israel, as he reigned as their King, and then through King David and his descendants—so that he might entrust the rule of creation to them again.

But the Old Testament story is a tragic one. Time and again, God's people failed to see how he was working to rescue them from their enemies, failed to submit to him as their King, and failed to see how he was going to crush the Serpent (as he promised Adam and Eve) and use them to bless the world (as he promised Abraham).

Already and Not Yet

While the Old Testament gives us hope and hints about God's work to establish his rule, save his people, and bring history to its ultimate end, it is only when we arrive in the New Testament that we begin to see his eschatological work clearly.

First of all, we see that Jesus talks about the kingdom both as having arrived and still yet to come. He says things like "If it is by the Spirit of God that I cast out demons, then the kingdom of God has come upon you" (Matt. 12:28) and "The kingdom of God is in the midst of you" (Luke 17:21b). But he also teaches us, in the Lord's Prayer, to pray that God's kingdom might come (Matt. 6:10). This means there is some aspect of the kingdom that is *already* present and some aspect that is still *not yet* fully here. We see this *already*-and-*not-yet* reality on display in other places in the New Testament. In fact, almost everything we read in the New Testament has a bit of an already-and-not-yet flavor to it. Have you ever noticed this?

You may have heard a pastor talk about how we have been saved, we are being saved, and we will be saved. This is because our redemption is already and not yet. On the one hand, it's clear that our redemption as Christians has already happened. Paul says that in Christ, "we have redemption, the forgiveness of sins" (Col. 1:14). On the other hand, he also talks about redemption as a future reality. In Romans 8:23b, he says, "We wait eagerly for adoption as sons, the redemption of our bodies." In some way, we are already experiencing while also waiting for redemption.

We can see the same reality when we talk about eternal life. In John's Gospel, Jesus says, "Whoever hears my word and believes him who sent me has eternal life" (5:24a). He does not say we will have eternal life someday, but that we have eternal life right now. But until Jesus returns, we all experience physical death. This is why Paul can talk about the day when God *will give* eternal life (Rom. 2:7) and how those who sow to the Spirit will reap eternal life from the Spirit (Gal. 6:8). The point is clear: eternal life is both already present but not yet here in its fullness.

Living in the Last Days

Another way of talking about the already and not yet is to say that we are living in the last days right now. Shortly after Jesus had ascended to heaven, Peter was preaching on the day of Pentecost. He told the crowd that had gathered around that the life, death, and resurrection of Jesus marked the beginning of the "last days," as the prophet Joel put it (Acts 2:17). Later in the New Testament, John writes, "Children, it is the last hour, and as you have heard that antichrist is coming, so now many antichrists have come" (1 John 2:18).

We could go on with examples that show how important it is to understand the already-and-not-yet principle—and, in some ways, I will do just that in the rest of this book. When we really understand the already-and-not-yet reality of the current age, it gives us confidence. God has worked and God will work. Because of what God has done for us in the past, we can be confident that he will work for us in the future. In fact, Paul says that the Holy Spirit is the down payment, or guarantee, that we will get our final inheritance (Eph. 1:14).

The German theologian Oscar Cullmann compared our time to the days between June 6, 1944, and May 7, 1945. Do you know what happened on those dates? On June 6—D-Day—and the days that followed, the Allied armies successfully invaded the European continent and began their advance to Berlin during World War II. At that point, the German forces were essentially defeated. But after the D-Day invasion, many more American, British, and French soldiers were killed in action. It was not until May 7, 1945, that the German armies finally surrendered.

While we are waiting for the completion of God's plan when Jesus returns in power, judges his enemies, and brings our final salvation in the new creation, we are living between the times. The turning point in history was the cross and resurrection. When Jesus went to the cross and then rose from the grave, he decisively defeated sin and death. The victory has already been won. But the final consummation of that victory has not yet come. In the meantime, we still feel the effects of sin and death, but we cannot forget that these are defeated enemies.

As we read our Bibles and look at these themes, we need to remember that we are living in the age of fulfillment—the last days, as Peter put it. The Old Testament promises have been fulfilled in and through Christ. But there is still much more yet to come.

Connecting Verses

Old Testament: Genesis 3:15
New Testament: Revelation 21:3–5

Summary Statement

To know the whole message of the Bible, we must know that God's end-time promises have already begun to be fulfilled through Jesus, but they are not yet complete, and will not be until Jesus returns to make all things new.

2

GOD

I probably have a modern Western bias, but I think one of the greatest characters in the history of literature is Bilbo Baggins. In *The Hobbit*, J. R. R. Tolkien masterfully describes Bilbo's character as it develops and strengthens in front of our eyes. At the beginning of the book, we are told that Bilbo comes from a family that "never had any adventures or did anything unexpected: you could tell what a Baggins would say on any question without the bother of asking him."[2] But we learn much more about Bilbo as the story unfolds, and by the end of the book, Bilbo does quite a few unexpected things—everything from saving his friends from giant spiders to matching wits with a fire-breathing dragon.

In a similar way, we don't learn everything about God on the first page of the Bible. As the grand narrative of redemptive history unfolds, we see far more than we do in the opening pages of Genesis. Unlike the story of Bilbo Baggins, however, what we see in the Bible is not the gradual transformation of a character into a hero. Instead, we see the gradual revelation of the standard for all other heroes. This is why *God* is the second word we must consider as we trace the message of the Bible.

God Is Our Creator and King

In the very first verses in the Bible, we see a clear picture of who God is: "In the beginning, God created the heavens and the earth" (Gen. 1:1). At his command, light, stars, water, dry land, and everything else came into being. Even if you did not go to Sunday school, that verse probably sounds familiar to you. It shows that God created all things simply by speaking them into existence. In fact, in Hebrews 11:3, we see even more clearly that God created all things by his word, "so that what is seen was not made out of things that are visible." If you ever hear theologians talking about creation *ex nihilo* ("out of nothing"), this is what they mean.

Not only did God create all things, but he is also in charge of all things. As the Psalms say many times over, God is on his throne, ruling over all his creation.[3] Back in Genesis, we can see he is in charge of his creation because he had authority to pronounce it good (Gen. 1:31). Then he entrusted the care of his creation to Adam and Eve. He is the King, and he entrusted his kingdom to us. That one did not turn out too well—or so it seemed. But our sin does not undermine God's right to reign or his majesty as King. He does not need us to rule the world. So we can also see that God's self-sufficiency is an important implication of his rightful place as Creator and King.

God Is Self-Sufficient

Have you ever thought about God's self-sufficiency? Theologians used to call it his aseity, which means, "from himself."

All God needs is from himself. But we are dependent beings. No plant created itself. The dry land did not appear before God commanded it to. And human beings would not exist apart from God speaking us into being.

Creation, then, teaches us that God is completely self-sufficient. If the universe thundered into being when he told it to, how could God lack for anything? The psalmist conveys the words of God: "If I were hungry, I would not tell you, for the world and its fullness are mine" (Ps. 50:12).

Despite this lesson from creation, it is easy for us to think that God needs *us*. Well-meaning Christians sometimes think that God created the world, and especially people, because he needed companionship, kind of like an elderly woman who gets a cat to keep her company. But in spite of what we might like to think, God does not need us. In Acts 17, Paul told the philosophers in Athens, "The God who made the world and everything in it, being Lord of heaven and earth, does not live in temples made by man, nor is he served by human hands, as though he needed anything, since he himself gives to all mankind life and breath and everything" (vv. 24–25). He does not need us. But we desperately need him. And he has decided to show us mercy.

The famous American pastor and theologian Jonathan Edwards wrote, "It is no argument of the emptiness or deficiency of a fountain that it is inclined to overflow."[4] What he means is that we never look at an overflowing fountain and think: "That fountain sure was missing something. It really needed dry ground to spill some water on." If anything, we think just the opposite—that the fountain had not a lack but an abundance! And this is how God is for us. He does not lack anything, but he overflows in mercy to us! As we move through the story of the Bible, we see that dependency always remains a one-way street.

God simply does not need us, but we desperately need him, because without his gracious intervention in history, we would be in serious trouble.

God Is Our Judge

After God entrusted his kingdom to Adam and Eve, they quickly disobeyed him and ate the fruit, as we saw in chapter 1. So he cursed the ground and sentenced them to death. Do you think this was rather harsh?

But consider what Adam and Eve did (Genesis 3). The God who had created them and provided for their every need also gave them a simple directive: do not eat from the tree of the knowledge of good and evil. But rather than trusting God's kindness to them, they doubted him and assumed they knew better. This was not an innocent mistake—it was a deliberate rejection of God's authority over them. It was nothing short of treason against the God who had made them. So he had every right to judge them. It would have been entirely just for God to wipe them out then and there. But he did not. While they still had to face the consequences of their sin, God showed them mercy even in the midst of his judgment, promising to crush the head of the Serpent one day (v. 15). So in judgment of sin, God also showed mercy to his people.

Many people have a picture of God as a vindictive judge, waiting to pounce on us as soon as we step out of line. But in reality, God's judgment of sin should give us hope. Think about it. There is so much evil and pain in the world. On the day I'm writing this, I've already heard about ongoing terrorism in the Middle East, including terrible persecution of Christians; the suicide of a well-known actor; and some nasty flooding in my hometown. If we believe that this is just the way it is and that there is no hope for justice, for peace, for God setting things right again, then not only will we tend toward depression, but we also will deny some of the most important teachings of the Bible. Hebrews 12:23 tells us that God is the Judge of all. Even though this is a serious warning, it should also give us hope.

God Is Our Covenant-Keeping Redeemer

When she is teaching new writers how to develop a plot, author Anne Lamott tells them not to give much attention to the plot. Instead, she tells them to focus on the relationships between their characters: "The development of relationship creates plot."[5] We can learn something important about the story of the Bible and the character of God from this observation.

Even in the midst of their sin and failure, God was committed to his people. In fact, this relationship between God and his creation helps us understand the unfolding plot of the Bible. In the moments after the first sin in the garden of Eden, God promised to crush the Serpent's head. Likewise, after he saved Noah and his family in the flood, God made a promise to his people and gave them a sign to remember his promise—the rainbow.

In the Bible, God makes promises in the form of covenants. For this reason, he often makes covenants with his people involving their need for redemption. We see this theme over and over again in the Bible. He promised to bless all the families of the earth through Abraham (Gen. 12:3). He also gave Abraham's descendants, Israel, the law to teach them about his standard for holiness and the need for a substitute in the sacrifices. He pledged that through David's family, he would establish an eternal kingdom. Even though God's people broke each of these covenants, he promised to send his servant and his Spirit to establish a new covenant.

God kept all of those promises through Jesus, the true seed of Abraham (Gal. 3:16), the One who obeyed God perfectly (2 Cor. 5:21) and became the substitutionary sacrifice to which the law was always pointing (Heb. 10:1–10). He is the Son of David, who will reign forever, and the servant who brings the promised Spirit. Through Jesus, God's relationship with his people is secure—both now and forever.

God Is Committed to His Own Glory

When Paul summarizes God's great plan of salvation in Romans 9–11, he concludes with an emphasis on God's glory: "For from him and through him and to him are all things. To him be glory forever. Amen" (Rom. 11:36). The picture of God throughout the story of the Bible can lead to only one conclusion: our Creator and King, the self-sufficient One, the Judge of all the earth, our covenant-keeping Redeemer, ought to be worshiped and honored. When you boil it down, the story of the Bible is a story about the glory of God and the joy of his people.

But that might raise a question in your mind. If you or I were to say that the history of the world is about our glory, it would be ridiculous, wouldn't it? So why is it not ridiculous for God to say that the history of redemption and the universe itself is all about his glory? He can say this because he actually is the most glorious thing in the universe, and delighting in him actually is the best thing for us. In fact, if he did not point us to his glory and invite us to worship him, then he would actually be *unloving*. God invites us into the glorious story of his glory on display, and the primary way he does this is through our redemption in Jesus.

So at this point, we have answered—at least in part—two crucial questions that are foundational for the rest of the book:

Who is God, and what has he done? In short, God is committed to his own glory, and he has intervened through Jesus to bring all of history to its intended goal. With these two foundational strands in place, we are ready to add three themes that help us frame the overall structure of the message of the Bible.

Connecting Verses

Old Testament: Psalm 50:9–12
New Testament: Romans 11:36

Summary Statement

To know the whole message of the Bible, we must know that God is our self-sufficient Creator and King, who judges sin and redeems his people through Jesus for the sake of his own glory.

PART 2

THE
FRAME

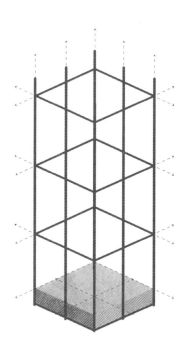

3

CREATION

Some people like to create things with their hands—like buildings or furniture or meals. My oldest son is an aspiring chef, and he's starting to make some fairly good dishes. I'm always happy to taste his creations, but I can't really make anything good myself—except maybe smoothies. On the other hand, I like to write, teach, and work toward ministry partnerships. My wife, Katie, likes to create lesson plans and strategies for school.

The things that give us fulfillment often involve bringing some kind of order out of chaos. In other words, they are ways of creating. For example, cooking involves taking seemingly random piles of ingredients and making something delicious out of them. The fact that we like to create shouldn't surprise us too much, because we human beings are made in the image of God, and as we saw in the last chapter, God is *the* Creator.

Creation and New Creation
We don't often go far beyond Genesis 1–2 when thinking about God's creative power. But creation is not simply a theme in the

first couple of chapters of the Bible. While it certainly begins in Genesis, the creation theme stretches through the whole Bible and becomes an important way of talking about how God works in history. God is the One who creates life where the only reasonable expectation is death and brings joy when all we can see is chaos. After all, he is the One who brought everything that now exists into being out of nothing.

The opening words of the Bible give us a glimpse into the creative power of God: "In the beginning, God created the heavens and the earth" (Gen. 1:1). But we see a little more about creation in the second verse—and this helps us understand what God is doing throughout the Bible. Apparently, after the initial moment of creation, the earth was a big mess. It was "without form and void" or, as Eugene Peterson puts it, "a soup of nothingness, a bottomless emptiness" (v. 2, MESSAGE). We don't know exactly what it looked like, but it was chaos. And during the rest of the creation week, God transformed that chaos into his good and orderly creation. He then commissioned his people, Adam and Eve, to be fruitful and fill the earth (v. 28). But God's creative work did not stop then.

After the human race continually rebelled against him, God judged his creation with the flood, reducing the earth to chaos again. Then, once more, God brought order out of chaos. In fact, if you read Genesis 8–9 carefully, you'll see a lot of the same language that you see in Genesis 1.

In Genesis 1:2, there was darkness over the face of the deep, and God's Spirit was hovering over the face of the waters. In Genesis 8:1, the "wind" (from the same Hebrew word translated as "Spirit") blew over the waters of the earth. Genesis 1:9 tells us how God gathered the waters so that the dry ground appeared, and Genesis 8:5 tells us that the tops of the mountains appeared first after the flood. Birds and then land animals are present in both Genesis 1:20–25 and Genesis 8:6–19. Finally, after Noah came out of the ark, God blessed him and commanded him to be fruitful and fill the earth (Gen. 9:1). It was like a new creation.[6] Even though Adam and Eve brought sin into the world, God promised to fix all that had gone wrong. Even after the chaos that the flood brought, God was not going to abandon his saving promises.

Both in the first creation and in the days after the flood, God turned chaos into order and darkness into light. But just as they did after the original creation, God's people failed to obey him. Shortly after he got off the ark, Noah got rip-roaring drunk, and his son Ham mocked him for it (Gen. 9:21–22). Noah and his son quickly demonstrated that sin was still a problem to be reckoned with. Even though Noah sinned, God still was committed to bringing order out of the chaos that sin brings. He was committed to his new creation.

Israel's New Creation

Long after the flood, God chose Noah's descendant Abraham and his family as his covenant people—the family he would use to bless the nations. But several generations down the line, Abraham's descendants—the people of Israel—found themselves enslaved in Egypt. It looked as if God's promises were on shaky ground, but God was committed to Abraham's family and would rescue them from slavery. He did it by bringing ten plagues on Egypt.

In these plagues, God was again bringing judgment that led to chaos. Instead of animals coming to life, we see animals dying. Instead of water being sent to its proper place, water was turned to blood. Instead of light appearing, the ninth plague covered the land in darkness. So the plagues were a kind of "uncreation."

But when God delivered Israel, it was like a new creation. When Israel came to the Red Sea on their way out of Egypt, a wind from God blew over the sea and divided the waters (Ex. 14:21; 15:8), so that dry land appeared—much like what happened in Genesis 1:9.

These themes are not accidental. In fact, the parallels continued after Israel passed through the Red Sea. The tabernacle that God commanded his people to build reminds us a little of the garden of Eden. We'll come back to that later, but notice that when it was built, everything was done as the Lord had commanded (Ex. 40:16)—just as the first creation was what God had intended it to be. Some scholars even argue that the seven speeches in Exodus 25–31 point us back to the seven days of creation! Whether that is true or not, the picture is basically clear—when God called his people out of Egypt, he reminded them that he brings order out of chaos to save his people.

Sadly, like Adam and Eve, Israel also rebelled against God's loving rule. After he delivered them from Egypt, God brought them to Mount Sinai. While they were waiting for Moses to come down from meeting with God on the mountain, the people got impatient. They weren't sure whether Moses was alive or dead. Like Adam and Eve, they tried to take matters into their own hands. Moses's brother, Aaron, agreed to go along with their rebellion and collected everyone's jewelry to make the infamous golden calf. And just like that, they had a god of their own ready to go.

Are you starting to see a pattern? Every time God brought order out of chaos in these "new creations," his people failed to trust him and immediately started running headlong back toward chaos. And so it continued throughout Israel's history—even though he had created a people, graciously given them his Word in the law, and provided them with a place to live in the Promised Land, they continued to turn their backs on him and look for security in other gods. Finally, God sent Assyria and Babylon to conquer Israel and take many of them captive.

The prophets sometimes describe Israel's exile as a type of chaos or "un-creation." When the prophet Jeremiah is describing what Judah will look like after the exile, he says, "I looked on the earth, and behold, it was without form and void; and to the heavens, and they had no light" (Jer. 4:23). The echoes of Genesis 1:2 are loud and clear.

Even though the exile was another return to chaos, God had promised to undo all the chaos that sin had brought into the world. This is why we also see the prophets pointing us back to creation. In fact, in Isaiah's prophecies, it is sometimes hard to tell whether God is talking about the creation of the universe or the new creation, when he will save his people. Sometimes he is talking about creating all things (as in Isa. 40:28), sometimes he is specifically talking about creating Israel (as in Isa. 43:15), and sometimes he is pointing to his promised renewal of the whole earth (as in Isa. 65:17). These are all clumped together because God wants us to see all of these things through the same lens: God's creative power.

After the exile, the Israelites did not make golden calves anymore, yet they continued to rebel against God. In the New Testament, Paul says that they were "ignorant of the righteousness of God, and seeking to establish their own" (Rom. 10:3). They were still running toward chaos.

New Creation Has Come

In 2 Corinthians 5:17, Paul writes, "If anyone is in Christ, he is a new creation." But the phrase that the English Standard Version translates as "he is a new creation" is a little more ambiguous in Paul's original Greek. The verse actually reads something like this: "If anyone is in Christ, new creation." It seems as if Paul is making a general statement about the new creation. That's why I like the New International Version translation: "Therefore, if anyone is in Christ, the new creation has come" (NIV). In other words, Paul is saying that when someone is united by faith to Christ, that is an evidence that the new creation has dawned. When you stop and think about it, this is a fairly amazing thing to say. Paul is saying that when Christians are united with Christ in his death and resurrection, this is a demonstration that God is keeping his promises to make all things new. How can he say this?

Paul can say there is a new creation because Jesus died and rose again. At the cross, we see another "uncreation." There was darkness instead of light, death instead of life. But on the other side of that chaos, Jesus emerged from the grave. In his resurrection, Jesus defeated sin and death once and for all. After all the other acts of creation in the Bible, it does not take long for sin and death to come storming back. In the garden, after the flood, at Mount Sinai, and after the exile, sin and death kept coming. But when Jesus rose from the dead, death was a defeated enemy.

And God's new creative work does not stop with Jesus. We saw earlier that the end-of-time creative work of God has burst into the present. That is why Paul can say that when someone believes in Christ, it is an evidence of the new creation. Earlier in 2 Corinthians, Paul writes, "God, who said, 'Let light shine out of darkness,' has shone in our hearts to give the light of the knowledge of the glory of God in the face of Jesus Christ" (4:6). Paul is talking about the new birth in a way that reminds us of God's first work of creation.

When God makes all things new, we will see this culmination of new creation. Even though we see God's promised new creation already fulfilled in the resurrection of Jesus and the salvation of individuals, we do not yet see the new creation fully. But we do have a picture of it in the text we saw earlier, Revelation 21. There we see God finally undoing the pain, sin, sickness, and death that the fall brought to the universe. Then God will truly make all things new. Just as it is in the history of redemption, God's creative power will be on display through all of eternity when he restores his creation.

Connecting Verses
Old Testament: Isaiah 65:17
New Testament: Revelation 21:1–5

Summary Statement
To know the whole message of the Bible, we must know that the Creator God, who brings order out of chaos, is making all things new through his Son, Jesus—both now, in the salvation of sinners, and finally in the new heaven and earth.

4

COVENANT

Most of us probably don't have a good understanding of covenantal relationships. Even if we don't come right out and say it, we tend to think of our relationships in contractual terms: "You give me this service and I'll give you these goods." The relationships are built around the philosophy of "What have you done for me lately?" But in the Bible, we find a different kind of relationship: a covenant.[7]

While it is a little hard to define a covenant in the Bible, it is something like "a relational promise marked by faithful love." It is relational. This means that it is not simply a cold business contract. The parties of the covenant know and care for each other in some meaningful sense. It is also a promise. A covenant is more than just a warm, fuzzy feeling. One person or group actually agrees to something, and another person or group agrees to something else. Finally, it is marked by faithful love. Both parties agree to be faithful to the terms of the covenant because there is a genuine and lasting love commitment between them. While this language probably brings the marriage covenant to your mind, every covenant should include this type of commitment.

Conditional and Unconditional Covenants?

Through the years, many scholars have debated what kind of covenants we find in the ancient world and how they work. They often talk in terms of conditional versus unconditional or gift versus obligation covenants, along with many other terms—such as a "suzerain-vassal covenant" (that's a fun one). We could spend a lot of time and energy debating the differences among ancient Near Eastern covenants, and I think there is a lot of value in those conversations. But I'm not convinced that it is best to understand biblical covenants as either *completely* conditional or *completely* unconditional.

For example, many scholars argue that the covenant that God made with Israel at Mount Sinai was a conditional covenant that required strict obedience. If the Israelites did not obey the terms of the covenant, they would face judgment. If they did obey, they would be blessed. When you read a passage such as Deuteronomy 27–28, it is hard to argue with this description. Compare Deuteronomy 27:15–26 with 28:1–5. If you don't keep the covenant, you are cursed. If you do, you are blessed. Seems rather cut and dried, right?

Well, if you keep reading into Deuteronomy 30, God says that after the blessing and the curse have come upon Israel, they will return to the Lord and he will pour out his blessing on them and "circumcise your heart and the heart of your offspring, so that you will love the LORD your God" (v. 6). In other words, God will make his people able to love him. As you keep reading this chapter, it becomes clear that the result of this will be abundant blessing. God is making an unconditional promise that the conditional aspects of this covenant will be fulfilled. Even though this covenant is certainly full of conditions, there is an unconditional aspect to the fulfillment of these conditions.

Many people also argue that the Abrahamic covenant was unconditional. That is to say, all of the blessings promised to Abraham in Genesis 15:1–6 would be given to him and his children regardless of whether they remained faithful to the covenant or not. But if you read the story of Abraham closely, it is not so simple. When God reiterates his covenant promises in Genesis 17, he also requires Abraham and his male family members to be circumcised. In other words, if they want to receive the promises of this unconditional covenant, they need to keep the condition of circumcision.

As you read the biblical covenants, I think that it is important to keep this tension between the conditional and unconditional in mind. God makes covenant promises to his people, but these come with conditions that must be met. As we understand the fulfillment of these conditions, we see the gospel and the story of the Bible clearly.

The First Covenant

Although you may not see it at first, the first covenant in the Bible is found in the first few chapters. If we look back at our definition of a covenant, it is clear that all of the elements were there. God and human beings were in a relationship and made promises to each other. Adam and Eve were to be fruitful, multiply, fill the earth, and care for it (Gen. 1:28). They were to rule on God's behalf in the garden of Eden. They also promised to be loyal to God by avoiding the tree of the knowledge of good and evil. God committed to caring for human beings, specifically by providing for them and all of his creation (v. 29).

After the flood, Moses confirmed that God's relationship with Adam and Eve in the garden was actually a covenant. This might get a little technical, but you signed up to go a little deeper! Anyway, in the Old Testament, the Hebrew word that means "cut" is typically used when an author is talking about making a covenant. To make a covenant is "to cut a covenant." But when the writers are talking about a covenant that has already been made, the typical word is "establish." So in Genesis 9:9, when God told Noah, "Behold, I establish my covenant with you," he was pointing to a covenant that had already been made. If you are wondering what covenant that might be, look back at my overview of all the similarities between Adam and Noah in chapter 3.

From the beginning, God committed himself to caring for and sustaining humanity and his creation with a covenant. But Adam and Eve, Noah, and everyone in between failed to keep this covenant. Because they broke that covenant relationship, sin and death were in the world. But God remained faithful, even though the human race did not. And that set the stage for what came next.

The Covenant with Abraham

The next major covenant we encounter is the covenant with Abraham. But we can't read this covenant apart from that first covenant. As the covenants in the Bible unfolded, they built on one another. Because God was still committed to keeping his covenant with creation, he came to Abraham with a promise to bless all of the families of the earth through him (Gen. 12:3). In other words, God was going to keep that first covenant by keeping the covenant with Abraham.

We have already seen that both God and Abraham had responsibilities in this covenant. God promised a land and many descendants. Best of all, God promised to bless Abraham by making him into a great nation that would bless the earth. Abraham was responsible for receiving the covenant sign of circumcision and the obedience that this sign implied. But in Genesis 15, we see an amazing twist.

In Abraham's day, when people talked about "cutting a covenant," they meant it quite literally. They would sacrifice an animal and cut it in half. Then the people making the covenant would walk between the animal parts together as a pledge of their covenant loyalty. By doing this, they were effectively saying, "If I don't keep this covenant, then you can do to me what we've done to this animal." It was serious business. Notice, though, what God did. Instead of God and Abraham passing through together, a smoldering pot and a flaming torch passed through the animal pieces alone (Gen. 15:17). This was a way of saying that God alone was taking both sides of the covenant promises on himself. He was saying that if Abraham and his family did not keep their promises, *he* would take the penalty for their sin on himself. He would pay the price they deserved for their disloyalty. These were high stakes—God pledged himself to pay the penalty an unfaithful people deserved!

The Covenant with Israel

After he brought the Israelites out of their slavery in Egypt, God led them to Mount Sinai, where he made another covenant with them. This covenant is often called the Mosaic law or just the law. Remember, God did not give the law to a random nation in the ancient Near East. The nation of Israel was Abraham's family. And God had promised to bless all nations through them.

We are going to think about the law in more detail a little

later, but right now we can summarize how it built on the covenants that came before and set the stage for what would come after it. Anyone who knows much about the Bible is aware that the law is full of rules and regulations. It is not hard to see that this covenant certainly had many conditions attached to it. But even within the covenant itself, there was the assumption that the covenant would be broken. The entire sacrificial system was a way to deal with the inevitable failure of the people to keep the law.

So the law covenant itself reveals that God's people would not keep the covenant. It may seem a little paradoxical, but think about what Paul says in Romans 5:20: "the law came in to increase the trespass." The covenant itself teaches us about our inability to keep the covenant. If I can put it bluntly, this covenant was designed to fail. Israel would not be able to keep its commission to bless the nations, and this would lead to eventual punishment in the form of exile to Assyria and Babylon. But God was still committed to keeping both sides of the covenant. The question was, how would he do it?

The Covenant with David

When Israel finally settled in the land God had promised Abraham, God made a special covenant with David, the king he chose to rule Israel. In this covenant, God promised that David's kingdom would last forever (2 Sam. 7:12–13) so that he could be a blessing to all nations (Ps. 72:17). God promised to bless all the nations through the line of David because it was through the kingdom of David that the rule and authority God had entrusted to Adam and Eve would be reestablished. Even though Israel as a whole was supposed to bring this blessing to the nations, the king had a special responsibility to represent the nation, just as an ambassador represents and speaks for his nation and its interests and responsibilities.

But as was the case with the other covenants in the Bible, God also required that David and his descendants stay faithful to the covenant or face discipline (2 Sam. 7:14). Just as the whole nation failed to keep the law, David's descendants failed to bring God's blessing to the nations. Then God sent prophets to proclaim that a king greater than David or his son Solomon would come to rule in the way God demanded, and thereby bless all the nations. God was still faithful to his promises. But for the moment, the covenant with David, like the covenants before it, did not have a faithful human partner.

The New Covenant

In spite of the failure of God's people to keep his covenants, God did not relent in his covenant commitment to his people and to the world. So he sent his prophets to tell of a greater covenant, in which all of the covenant promises would finally be kept. The basics of this covenant were the same as in the ones we have seen so far. God promised to bless his people and the world. But this covenant was different, because this time God also promised that his people would keep the covenant.

The descriptions of this new covenant (as it is usually called) are nothing short of miraculous. In Isaiah, we see that God promised to send a truly faithful king from the line of David to bless all the earth with the knowledge and presence of the true God (Isa. 11:9). Isaiah also spoke of a servant who would take the penalty of God's people—the judgment that their covenant breaking deserved—on his own shoulders (Isa. 53:6). The result of this would be the new creation that we saw in the last chapter. Jeremiah looked forward to the day when the house of Israel and the house of Judah (God's reunited people) would keep the covenant because God promised, "I will put my law within them, and I will write it on their hearts" (Jer. 31:33). He would give his people the ability to keep the covenant. Ezekiel spoke of a day when God would breathe new life into his people, overcoming death as the consequence for sin (Ezek. 37:6). On and on we could go, but the bottom line is that the prophets looked forward to a day when God would finally and fully keep his covenant promises.

Jesus, Our Covenant King

Each covenant in the Old Testament not only builds on what has gone before, but also ratchets up the anticipation. As God unfolds each covenant, we are always wondering whether this will be the one to fulfill all of the promises. When we arrive in the New Testament, we discover that Jesus is the One who fulfills all of the covenant conditions perfectly.

He is the Davidic King who blesses the nations. He takes the curse of the law on himself, fulfilling God's commitment to take the covenant penalties alone. He keeps the law perfectly so that all who are united to him have the law written on their hearts. He defeats death through his resurrection from the dead. He is the One who does what Adam, Noah, Abraham, Israel, David, and everyone else failed to do: perfectly keep the requirements of the covenants. As a result, Paul tells us, "All the promises of God find their Yes in him" (2 Cor. 1:20). As Jesus fulfills God's covenant promises, God's saving rule and reign move forward. But we are still living in the already-and-not-yet new covenant age, where God's kingdom is on the move but not yet present the way it will be at the end. And that leads us to our next key theme, the kingdom of God.

Connecting Verses

Old Testament: Jeremiah 31:31–34
New Testament: Hebrews 9:13–15

Summary Statement

To know the whole message of the Bible, we must know that God always relates to his people through covenants, all of which are fulfilled in Jesus the Messiah.

5

KINGDOM

If you asked a room full of Christians to explain what the Bible means by "the kingdom of God," you would probably get quite a few different answers—even if they were all members of the same church!

Some might say the kingdom of God is the church. Others might say it is the nation of Israel. Some could be thinking about different Christian ministries, and some might think the kingdom is wherever we can sense the presence of God. Probably quite a few would say the kingdom of God is something to look forward to at the end of history. A lot of other people (and maybe even some of the same people) might say that the kingdom of God is something we can experience here and now.

We could go on listing different ways to describe the kingdom, but the truth is, while the Bible does talk about the kingdom of God in different ways, these ways might not always be what we think they are. So we need to start by explaining a little bit about what the term "kingdom of God" actually means.

God's Saving Reign

If I were to talk to you about the kingdom of Saudi Arabia, you'd have a fairly good idea of what I mean. I'd be talking about the nation-state of Saudi Arabia, the country that fills most of the Arabian Peninsula and is bordered by Iraq to the north and Yemen to the south. When we think about kingdoms, we tend to think in these geopolitical terms. But these terms do not quite give the whole picture when we talk about the kingdom in the Bible.

When the Bible talks about God's kingdom, it is not talking first and foremost about a land with borders and a centralized government. Instead, it is talking first about God's power and authority to rule. But this does not mean that we cannot ever talk about a particular place when we are talking about God's kingdom (or any other kingdom for that matter). After all, the existence of a ruler implies a place where he rules.

Think of it this way: if I'm talking about the "United Kingdom of Great Britain and Northern Ireland," then I'm assuming that this kingdom has a monarch. As I'm writing this, the monarch of this particular kingdom, Queen Elizabeth II, recently became the longest reigning British monarch in history.

Don't push too hard on this analogy, however, because the powers of the British monarchy aren't exactly what they used to be. With the kingdom of God, we can be sure that the authority of its Ruler has not decreased in any way, shape, or form. But whether we are talking about a constitutional monarch, such as the queen of England; an absolute monarch, such as the king of Saudi Arabia; or the King of kings, we cannot separate a monarch from his or her authority as ruler. What this all means is that when we think about the kingdom of God, we need to start with God's active authority to rule.

Your Kingdom Come?

At this point, you might be thinking about the petition in the Lord's Prayer that we mentioned earlier, where Jesus teaches us to pray that God's kingdom will come. If so, you might also be wondering how I can define the kingdom of God as God's authority to rule. After all, Psalm 103:19 says, "The LORD has established his throne in the heavens, and his kingdom rules over all." How can we pray that God's kingdom will come if his kingdom rules over all?

To answer this, we need to see that the Bible actually talks about the kingdom of God in two ways. Verses such as Psalm 103:19 point us to God's sovereign rule over all things. Also, Psalm 47:7–8 says: "God is the King of all the earth; sing praises with a psalm! God reigns over the nations; God sits on his holy throne." It is clear that God is reigning over all things right now in some way.

To see a second way the Bible talks about the kingdom, let's think about the story of the Bible in the Lord's Prayer (Matt. 6:9–13). Don't misunderstand me—I'm not saying that the Lord's Prayer is a story in and of itself. But when we read it through the lens of the wider story of the Bible, we can see that the kingdom of God in the story of Scripture should shape the way we read this prayer.

Jesus begins the prayer by asking that the name of God, our heavenly Father, would be "hallowed," or honored (v. 9). There is a lot of truth about God as Father and the glory of his name packed into that petition. Before we talk about the kingdom, let's not forget that the kingdom is all about the King. Remember, the universe itself exists for God's glory. But as Jesus continues to pray, we see what it looks like for God's name to be honored: "Your kingdom come, your will be done, on earth as it is in heaven" (v. 10).

In short, God's name is glorified when his kingdom comes, and his kingdom comes when his will is done on earth just as it is in heaven. This helps us understand the second way the Bible talks about the kingdom of God. If we start by thinking about how God's will is done in heaven, the rest of the definition works itself out from there. In heaven, God's will is done perfectly. All of the angels and the other heavenly beings are in perfect submission to him. When we get a little glimpse of the throne room of heaven in passages such as Isaiah 6 or Revelation 4, we see a place where every being recognizes the glory and supremacy of God.

Jesus is teaching that when we pray for God's kingdom to come, we are praying that the earth and everyone in it will be in full and complete submission to him. We are praying for God to undo the results of sin and to defeat death. We are praying that the new creation will come. Then the reign of God will be plain for all to see.

But Jesus talks about the kingdom as both already present and not yet fully here. This is because God has already started bringing the earth into submission and restoring the world to its original glory—but there is much more to come.

At the beginning of creation, God installed Adam and Eve as king and queen. Remember, they were supposed to subdue the earth and have dominion over it (Gen. 1:28). If you have ever read The Chronicles of Narnia, you have seen how C. S. Lewis paints a picture of what this kind of rule looks like. Aslan is the king of Narnia, but Peter, Edmund, Susan, and Lucy are his representative rulers. They are to rule Narnia on Aslan's behalf. In the same way, Adam and Eve were to rule on God's behalf—but they failed to do this.

Even though Adam and Eve failed, causing sin and death to

enter the world, God determined to bring the whole creation back under his reign. He said that the offspring of Eve would defeat the Serpent and undo the curse (Gen. 3:15). He promised that all the families of the earth would be blessed through Abraham (Gen. 12:3) and that Abraham's great-grandson Judah would have a descendant who would rule the nations (Gen. 49:10). King David, the greatest king of Israel in the Old Testament, was a descendant of Judah. He brought God's rule over the realm of Israel. Even though David failed to obey God perfectly, God promised that he would have an even greater son, who would rule forever (2 Sam. 7:12–13) and bring blessing to the nations (Ps. 72:17). In other words, God promised to bless the whole world through the reign of this promised Son of David when the new covenant was established. We saw in the last chapter that God advances his saving plan through the covenants. Here we can add one more piece and say that God advances his kingdom through his covenants.[8]

The Gospel of the Kingdom

When Jesus came on the scene proclaiming the kingdom of God, he was announcing that the promised renewal was under way. And it began with his call for people to repent and believe the good news. As men and women turn away from their sin and cast themselves on Jesus, God's reign advances. That is why Jesus also teaches us to pray that God will provide our daily needs and forgive our sins (Matt. 6:11–12). When we pray these things, we are expressing our need for God and submission to him. He is the One who meets our needs. When we sin against him, we need his forgiveness. When others sin against us, we reflect his will by forgiving them rather than holding on to bitterness or anger. We seek his kingdom by fighting against sin when it wells up in our hearts. This defeat of our sin is rooted in the saving work of Jesus on the cross.

I like how Jeremy Treat summarizes this relationship: "The kingdom is the ultimate goal of the cross, and the cross is the means by which the kingdom comes."[9] When we say no to sin, we are demonstrating that the saving reign of God is present among us. That is why we can say that even though Paul, Peter, John, and the rest of the New Testament writers outside the Gospels don't use "kingdom language" very much, the kingdom of God was never far from their minds.

The kingdom of God advances as the good news goes forward. As more and more people turn away from their sin and put their trust in Jesus alone, the will of God is being done on earth as it is in heaven. As we live in the already and not yet, we need to keep praying and working so that God's saving reign goes forward. But we can also have confidence that our prayer will one day be answered in the greatest possible way.

Hundreds of years before Jesus was born, the prophet Habakkuk looked forward to a day when "the earth will be filled with the knowledge of the glory of the LORD as the waters cover the sea" (Hab. 2:14). The prophet Zechariah said that in that great day, "the LORD will be king over all the earth" (Zech. 14:9). In the New Testament, Paul speaks of a coming day when "all things are subjected" to Jesus and the Father (1 Cor. 15:28). And in the book of Revelation, John records his vision of the end of the age, when "the throne of God and of the Lamb" will be the center and source of their worldwide kingdom (Rev. 22:1). We can be sure that God's kingdom will come as the earth is renewed and transformed in submission to his perfect will. Then God's reign and God's realm will cover the entire creation. Looking forward to this day, we should be filled with hope regardless of how our present circumstances look.

In this second section of our journey, we've seen three key themes that should help us interpret the framework of the story of the Bible. Seeing creation, covenant, and kingdom as central strands in the message of the Bible should give us a better sense of the whole picture. We see a God who makes all things new moving his saving reign forward through his covenants. Because Jesus died and rose again, God's saving reign is present and advancing. And we can look forward to the day when he will finally make all things new.

With this structure in place, we are going to look at a series of themes that are intertwined with what we've seen so far. The remaining chapters will tell the story of the Bible, at least in part, as we trace the progressive development of each of these themes and highlight their culmination in the gospel of Jesus Christ.

Connecting Verses

Old Testament: Zechariah 14:9
New Testament: Matthew 6:10

Summary Statement

To know the whole message of the Bible, we must know that God reigns as King in his sovereign rule over creation, his salvation of sinners through Jesus, and his future rule over all the world in the new creation.

PART 3

THE
SUPERSTRUCTURE

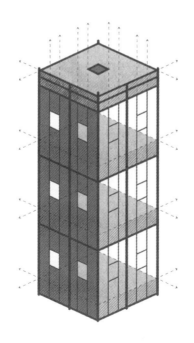

6

TEMPLE

If you are a Christian, you probably have heard someone say (or maybe you've said yourself) that the human body is a temple. Someone will turn down a dessert and say, "My body is a temple." Or when you work out, you'll say, "I've gotta take care of the temple."

But in the ancient world, most people had a different idea about what a temple was supposed to be. The temple wasn't you or something inside of you—it was very much outside of you. A temple was a brick-and-mortar (or stone, wood, or some other material) building in your village or another town. For millennia, the temple was the place you went to worship your god or gods.

The Garden Temple

If I were to ask you where we find the first temple in the Bible, you might point to King Solomon's temple (1 Kings 6–7) or maybe to the tabernacle (Exodus 26). You would be right to turn to those places. But I think we actually find the first temple in the first few chapters of the Bible, when God was present with his people in a special way.

Now you might be thinking, isn't God everywhere? The Bible teaches that God is present everywhere in some sense. For example, Jeremiah 23:24 says that God fills heaven and earth. But when we talk about God's presence in a temple, we are speaking about a unique kind of presence. It involves God talking with his people, teaching them about who he is. In fact, a temple indicates that God is *living* with his people. This is the kind of presence of God that we see in Genesis 3:8, when he came to walk with Adam and Eve in the cool part of the day. We could even say that the garden itself was a temple.

We've already mentioned Adam and Eve's commission to be fruitful, multiply, fill the earth, and subdue it (Gen. 1:28). What we have not really emphasized yet is that this commission meant that Adam and Eve's job was to expand the "garden temple," where God had chosen to put his unique presence. From the beginning, God was planning to fill the earth with his glorious presence. As we know, Adam failed, sin and death entered the world, and God evicted them from the garden, away from his presence.

But even after sin came into the world, God was still committed to living with his people in a special way, and he wanted his people to call others to share the blessing of his presence. In our overview of the biblical covenants in chapter 4, we saw that God was going to use Abraham's family to bless the world. As we think about God's presence in Israel, we can't lose sight of that larger mission.

Israel's Temple

So let's jump forward from the garden to ancient Egypt. After God rescued the people of Israel, Abraham's family, from slavery, he led them through the wilderness with his visible presence. Exodus tells us about a pillar of cloud that led the people during the day and a pillar of fire that led them during the night. Day and night, these pillars "did not depart from before the people" (Ex. 13:22). This is a clear display of God's grace. For the first time since the fall, God's unique presence was with his people again.

As part of the covenant that he gave them at Mount Sinai, God told the Israelites to build a tabernacle as the place for his presence to dwell during their time in the wilderness. After Israel settled in the Promised Land, God gave his people careful instructions for building a permanent temple to take the place of the tabernacle. God was specific about the materials, colors, sizes, and overall design of both the tabernacle and the temple, but I want to point out just two key features.

First, God told the Israelites to place the ark (usually we call this the "ark of the covenant") in the "Most Holy Place" of the temple, where he would meet with his people (Ex. 25:22). Don't let Indiana Jones twist your understanding of the ark of the covenant. There was nothing magical about the ark in and of itself. Instead, think about the bigger picture. God was giving his people instructions for a sanctuary so his presence could remain with them.

But God's presence was limited to just that place in the temple. It was the Most Holy Place, which only the high priest could enter only once a year, on the Day of Atonement. On this day, the high priest would offer sacrifices for himself and for the people as a reminder that their sin still kept God's presence at a distance. Even though God was with his people again, it was not the intimate presence that Adam and Eve had enjoyed in the garden. It was limited and largely inaccessible to the people.

Second, notice that the tabernacle and the temple were full

of floral and gardenlike designs. The golden lampstand (or menorah) in the tabernacle was made to look like a tree with almond blossoms (Ex. 25:31–40). The high priest had woven pomegranates on the hem of his robe (Ex. 28:34). The pillars of the later temple in Jerusalem were topped with engravings of pomegranates and lilies (1 Kings 7:18–19). A large pool of water outside the temple was designed to look like the flower of a lily (1 Kings 7:26).

You might be wondering why I'm making such a big deal out of the trimwork in the temple. After all, your grandmother might have lilies on her wallpaper, but it does not really mean anything.

Well, if you go back to Genesis 1–3, all of this garden imagery starts to make sense. The garden of Eden was the place where God lived among his people. The tree of life gives us a model for the lampstand. Eden was rich in the types of precious stones that were used to build the temple (Gen. 2:12). The prophet Ezekiel tells us that, like Solomon's temple, the garden was on "the holy mountain of God" (Ezek. 28:14).

The connections between Eden and the temple remind us that God is committed to fixing all that went wrong in the fall. He is working to restore his presence among his people. The temple also reminds us that God's intimate presence was not yet restored. It pointed back to the garden, but the limited presence of God in the temple pointed forward to a greater experience of the presence of God still to come.

Yet even this limited experience of God's presence was not going to last. In Ezekiel 10, the prophet describes a vision of God's glory leaving the temple as he sends Israel into exile. Tragically, rather than extending God's presence throughout the earth, Israel continued to disobey him, leading to the departure of his glorious presence from the temple. But this was not the last word.

The True Temple

Let's jump forward again, to around AD 30, outside of the Samaritan city of Sychar, about thirty-five miles north of Jerusalem. Here a Jewish rabbi is talking with a Samaritan woman near a well. In a not-so-subtle effort to deflect the conversation away from her own sin, the woman asks the rabbi, Jesus, about God's presence in the temple at Jerusalem. The Samaritans had set up a different temple in which to worship God, but Jesus confirms that the temple in Jerusalem is—or was—the place where God meets his people (John 4:22). Notice what he goes on to say in verse 23: "The hour is coming, and is now here, when true worshipers will worship the Father in spirit and truth." In other words, God's people no longer have to meet him in a particular *place*. Instead, they have to meet him in a particular *way*. This is revolutionary—Jesus is saying that God's special presence among his people is no longer limited to the temple. How in the world can he say this?

We can find part of the answer earlier in John's Gospel. In John 1:14, John tells us that Jesus, the living Word of God, became a human being and "dwelt among us." The word we translate as "dwelt" is fairly unusual. It is closely related to the Greek word for "tent" or "tabernacle." We could even say the Word became flesh and "*tabernacled*" among us. God himself came to live among his people.

Wherever Jesus is present, God himself is present. This is why Jesus could talk about his body as a temple (John 2:19). It is why Jesus could say that he is greater than Solomon (Matt. 12:42). Solomon built the first temple for God to live with his people, but Jesus himself brought the presence of God to his people in a new and greater way—he was the living tabernacle of God.

If we understand this, it should change the way we view the mission of the church. In the Great Commission (Matt. 28:19–20), Jesus told his followers to take the gospel to the ends of the earth. We can see the power and motivation behind this command at the end of verse 20: "I am with you always, to the end of the age." Do you see that? Jesus, who brought God's presence to his people, also sends his people on their mission with that same presence.

As we take the gospel to the ends of the earth, we are actually doing what Adam and Eve failed to do—expand the boundaries of God's temple so that it fills the earth. As the church is built, God's presence fills the earth. Paul can say we are God's temple in 1 Corinthians 3:16 because "God's Spirit dwells in [us]." This is also why Peter can say that we are "like living stones . . . being built up as a spiritual house" (1 Pet. 2:5). The point of the temple was to bring God's special presence to his people. As Jesus builds his church, that purpose is being fulfilled in new and greater ways. Our missions work is actually "temple-building," because we are bringing people to Jesus, the true temple.

Finally, as we've seen already, this building project is already under way but not yet finished. And it will not be finished until the end of this age, when God himself will make all things new. In the last chapters of the Bible, we get a glimpse of this day. In John's description of the new creation in Revelation 21, the New Jerusalem is a perfect square coming down from heaven, just as the Most Holy Place of the original temple was a perfect square (2 Chron. 3:8). This is another way of saying that God's presence, which was once limited to the most isolated room in the temple, will fill the entire new creation. The Lord himself will be the temple, the dwelling place of God will be with man, and the commission to Adam and Eve will finally be fulfilled. His glorious presence will fill all of creation, and his people will live with him forever. If that doesn't get you excited, then go back to page 1 and start over, because you are missing something!

Connecting Verses

Old Testament: Exodus 29:46
New Testament: Revelation 21:3

Summary Statement

To know the whole message of the Bible, we must understand that God is committed to dwelling with his people as Jesus "tabernacles" among us now and finally when the presence of God will fill the new creation.

7

MESSIAH

I don't know about you, but I'm not a big fan of waiting. When I was a kid, my extended family gathered every year on Christmas Eve to open presents. I remember sitting at my grandma's house, staring at the presents stacked under the tree and literally watching the seconds tick off the clock until the hour when we could finally start opening them. Usually the adults had mercy on my brother and me and let us open one present sometime earlier in the day. But more often than not, opening that one present just left us wanting more and made it even harder to wait for the rest of them. And the sad thing is, within a few days, we weren't that interested in the toys we opened (with a few exceptions, such as the Nintendo Power Pad or the G. I. Joe aircraft carrier). Most of the time, the anticipation didn't quite live up to the reality.

A good part of the story of the Bible involves God's people waiting. They waited for God to work, to keep his promises, to undo the curse, and to send his Promised One. Just as my parents let my brother and me open a present in the afternoon,

God gave his people tastes of the main event along the way. But these only increased their anticipation. Unlike my Christmas presents, though, the reality far surpassed the anticipation when the Promised One—Jesus the Messiah—finally came.

In this chapter, I want to point to several places in the Old Testament where God gave his people previews of the coming Messiah. Along the way, we will see how the promises progressively revealed God's plan throughout the Old Testament and how Jesus fulfilled them.

Adam

After Adam's failure in the garden of Eden, the world needed a cure for the curse, sin, and death. The first hint at this solution comes in Genesis 3:15, when God promised that the offspring of the woman would crush the Serpent's head. Even though the offspring of the Serpent and the offspring of the woman would be at war for centuries to come, the outcome of that battle was never in doubt. The offspring of the woman would win. But the rest of the Old Testament tells the story of God's people waiting for that Promised One.

In the New Testament, Paul calls Jesus "the last Adam" (1 Cor. 15:45). He is the One Genesis 3:15 is talking about—the offspring of the woman who would "reverse the curse." In his letter to the church at Rome, Paul also says that "by the one man's obedience the many will be made righteous" (Rom. 5:19). In other words, Jesus's obedience is necessary to reverse the outcome of Adam's disobedience. But how is it that one person's actions can count for another person? As we move through the story of the Old Testament, we learn more about how one person can represent a larger group. As we learn more about this, we learn more about the Promised One.

Abraham

We have already talked about Abraham quite a bit, and he will come up a few more times, so we need to look at only one passage right now. About twenty-five years after God first called him, while he was still waiting for his promised son, the Lord told Abraham, "I will establish my covenant between me and you and your offspring after you" (Gen. 17:7). From this time onward, God's saving promises were focused on Abraham and his offspring. But everyone who was a part of the covenant got to enjoy the promises as well. This is because they were connected to Abraham.

In the New Testament, Paul helps us see how significant this verse from Genesis really is. In Galatians 3:16, Paul says that promises were not given to many people but to one single person: Jesus the Messiah. When Jesus comes, the promises are given to him. And everyone who is connected to him by faith gets these promises as well. This is why Paul tells the Galatians, "If you are Christ's, then you are Abraham's offspring, heirs according to promise" (Gal. 3:29).

David

One thousand years after Abraham, the people of God were still waiting for the Promised One. They saw hints and pictures of this Promised One in the law and the need for sacrifices, but it was not until King David's time that they got more clarity about what it would look like for a single person to represent the people of God.

In the ancient world, the king of a particular nation was seen as the living embodiment of that nation. While this idea usually leads in some unhealthy directions (both for the ego of that monarch and the rights of his people), it is based on a sliver of truth. With Adam and Abraham, we've already seen how a single person can represent a larger group. This is taken to another level in God's promises to his king—both David and Jesus.

Abraham's grandson Jacob told his own son Judah that he would have a royal descendant who would one day rule the nations (Gen. 49:10). Hundreds of years later, God made a covenant with Judah's descendant, David, telling him that his offspring would receive a never-ending kingdom (2 Sam. 7:12–13).

In the Psalms, this Promised One is sometimes called the "Anointed One" (see, for example, Pss. 2:2; 20:6; 84:9). The Hebrew word used in these psalms is *Maschiach*, which is where we get the word *Messiah*. When this word is translated into Greek, it is *Xristos*, or *Christ*. When we refer to Jesus as Christ, it is another way of saying that he is the Promised One, the Son of David.

But let's not lose sight of the pattern we saw earlier: the promises are given to a single person, but the rest of the people of God get to share in those promises. In the New Testament, then, when Jesus reigns as King, we get to share in his rule. And we don't even have to go all the way to the New Testament to see this idea repeated.

In the book of Daniel, we meet a mysterious figure called "one like a son of man" (Dan. 7:13). God gives this figure authority to rule on an eternal throne. Seems simple enough, right? This is the fulfillment of the promise to David—this is the Promised One. But if we keep reading in Daniel 7, we also hear that "the saints of the Most High shall receive the kingdom and possess the kingdom forever" (v. 18). Which is it? Does the Son of Man get to rule? Or is it the saints?

The answer is both. Both the Son of Man and the saints are reigning. This is because the people of God get to share in what

God promised to the single person (in this case, the King). But just as the people were waiting for the Promised One, we are waiting for the return of the Promised One, Jesus, who will reign forever. This is why Paul can say, "If we endure, we will also reign with him" (2 Tim. 2:12). The King represents the people, and the people of God share in the reign of the King. Amazing!

The Suffering Servant

Maybe the most familiar Old Testament passage in which one person represents the people of God is the suffering servant prophecy in Isaiah 53 and the chapters that surround it. As we see what it looks like for the servant to suffer in the place of God's people, we are given one more picture of the Promised One in the Old Testament.

To see how the servant is both a single person and the representative of God's people, let's read Isaiah 49:3–5 carefully. First, the servant of the Lord is called Israel in verse 3. It seems as if the whole nation is the servant. But keep reading. In verse 5, he also gets the job of bringing Jacob (another name for Israel) back to the Lord so that "Israel might be gathered to him." In other words, Israel fulfills its role as servant when its single representative does what the whole nation did not—or could not—do. One person, the servant, represents Israel.

While God's people were waiting for the new Adam, the son of Abraham, and especially the King, the Messiah, not many of them saw that the Promised One was also going to suffer. This is what tripped up Jesus's disciples. When Jesus told him he was going to suffer and die, Peter said: "Far be it from you, Lord! This shall never happen to you" (Matt. 16:22). Jesus answered him about as harshly as you could imagine: "Get behind me, Satan! You are a hindrance to me. For you are not setting your mind on the things of God, but on the things of man" (v. 23). The disciples were looking for a conquering King, but they failed to see that he was also the suffering servant.

Decades later, Peter saw as clearly as anyone that Jesus was the servant. Peter gives a lot of attention to Jesus as the suffering servant (maybe with Jesus's stinging words still ringing in his ears). Peter points us back to Isaiah 53 when he writes: "He himself bore our sins in his body on the tree, that we might die to sin and live to righteousness. By his wounds you have been healed" (1 Pet. 2:24). But a few verses earlier, Peter also writes, "Christ also suffered for you, leaving you an example, so that you might follow in his steps" (v. 21). While there is a big difference between Jesus's suffering and ours (our suffering isn't going to save anyone from his or her sin), the New Testament is clear: if we have faith in Jesus, we are called to suffer for the sake of the world. The people of God are both united to the Promised One in suffering and called to imitate his mission of suffering.

Jesus the Messiah

Through the Old Testament, God was teaching his people about the Promised One while they were waiting for his salvation. When God promised that the offspring of Eve would crush the head of the Serpent, Adam and Eve probably could not have imagined all that this meant. But as the story of the Bible unfolds, we see that the Promised One is the last Adam, the offspring of Abraham, the King who rules on David's throne, and the suffering servant. When all of these threads are woven together, they create a rich picture of Jesus, who fulfills and finishes all that the people of God were promised to have and intended to be.

As Jesus fulfills the task of Adam, everyone who has faith in him receives the promise of life. As Jesus receives the promises to Abraham, the blessing of Abraham goes to everyone who is in Christ (Gal. 3:29). As Jesus reigns, so we will reign with him (2 Tim. 2:12). But as Jesus suffers, we are called to suffer with him (1 Pet. 2:21). Throughout the story of the Bible, we have a picture of a Promised One who represents the people of God so that they share in God's promises and in his ongoing mission in the world!

Connecting Verses

Old Testament: Genesis 17:7
New Testament: Galatians 3:16

Summary Statement

To know the whole message of the Bible, we must know that the promised Messiah overcomes the sin of Adam, receives the blessing of Abraham, reigns on the throne of David, and suffers to pay the penalty for God's people and represent everyone who believes in him.

8

ISRAEL

After spending years analyzing and describing happiness as a psychological phenomenon, Dr. Ed Diener, who is called "the world's leading expert on happiness" (at least on the back of his book), concluded, "Relationships matter to happiness and are a key part of psychological wealth."[10] I don't think most people would argue with this conclusion. To be honest, I'm not really sure what "psychological wealth" is, but Dr. Diener is right to say that relationships matter to happiness. You don't have to have a PhD in psychology—or really any special insight into human nature—to recognize that human beings function best in some kind of relational community.

But what does that have to do with the story of the Bible? Does the big picture of redemption have anything to teach us about why we long for community and what that community should look like? Yes! In the story of the Bible, we can see that God has called his people into a community—both now and for all of eternity.

Before we move forward, let me defend my use of the word *community*. A lot of people use *community* as a trendy way of talking about all kinds of relationships, from bowling leagues to Bible studies. We might even be tempted to say that the word does not mean much anymore. But I don't want to give it up just yet. It is a valuable word—it reminds us that when we are in *community* with someone, we have significant things in *common* with that person. When God calls us into community with himself and with each other, we experience far more than "psychological wealth."

Community of the Trinity

When we think about the community of God's people, we really have to start with the community that exists within God himself. Have you ever thought about that community? Christians believe there is one God who has always (and we mean *always*) existed as three persons: the Father, the Son, and the Holy Spirit. This means there has always been divine community—not the easiest thing to wrap your mind around.

Just before he went to the cross, Jesus prayed, "Father, glorify me in your own presence with the glory that I had with you before the world existed" (John 17:5). Jesus and the Father had some kind of community before the universe was created. Since he is the third member of the Trinity, the Holy Spirit must have shared in that experience as well. But later, Jesus prayed something even more incredible. He asked that everyone who believes in him "may all be one, just as you, Father, are in me, and I in you, that they also may be in us" (v. 21). Do you see what is going on here? Jesus is saying that everyone who believes in him is invited into the community of the Trinity!

Don't misunderstand—Jesus is not saying that all Christians

get to become part the Trinity. Instead, he is saying that everyone who believes in him experiences something that the members of the Trinity experience. The perfect unity between Father, Son, and Holy Spirit is a picture of what the people of God get to enjoy—with God himself, but also with each other. The call to follow Jesus has always been a call to be a part of his covenant people. And when God calls his people into a covenant with him, he also brings them together into a community.

Adam and Eve

If you have been to many weddings, there is a good chance you've heard a sermon from Genesis 2:18. God had made the animals and paired them together, but Adam was alone. So God said, "It is not good that the man should be alone; I will make him a helper fit for him." Now this verse does have a lot to teach us about marriage and God's design for a husband and wife to complement and complete each other. But it also teaches us about the need for God's people to live in community from the very beginning.

We've also seen that God created men and women in his image (Gen. 1:27), and part of what it means to be made in God's image is to rule on his behalf. But I think the community of the Trinity also helps us understand what it means to be made in God's image. At the very least, we have to say that God has existed in an eternal community; when God says in Genesis 2 that man should not be alone, his desire is for his people to experience something like the community of the Trinity.

But God did not call Adam and Eve into community with him so they could just sit and gaze at their navels. He also gave them a *commission* to be fruitful and fill the earth with his glory (Gen. 1:28). From the beginning, God called his people into community for the purpose of accomplishing his mission in the world. But sin ruptured that perfect community. When Adam and Eve hid from God (Gen. 3:8), it is clear that they were no longer living in harmony with him. Then Adam and Eve's son Cain killed his brother, Abel (Gen. 4:8). The community was imploding. But we know that God had promised to make it right one day.

Israel

As we move forward, think about the way God called his people into a community in the covenants with Abraham and Israel. In both of these covenants, God called them into a community that was distinct from the nations, but also commissioned to display God's glorious holiness to those nations.

We've already seen that Abraham and his family were called to be the instrument God used to bless all the families of the earth (Gen. 12:3). God also told Abraham to circumcise his son Isaac and every male in his household as a covenant sign (Gen. 17:10). It needed to be clear who was and was not a member of the covenant.

Remember that God's covenant with Israel was a way of continuing the mission of the covenant with Abraham. Just as he did for Abraham, God gave the Israelites circumcision as a sign that set them apart as members of his covenant (Lev. 12:3). Israel was set apart for the purpose of blessing the nations. In the book of Deuteronomy, which is a recap of the covenant with Israel, God told the people that they were holy, or set apart, to God (Deut. 7:6).

In Exodus 12, when he brought them out of slavery in Egypt, God gave the Israelites another way to remember his covenant with them. The ten plagues that God sent to Egypt culminated with the death of every firstborn son in the land. But God promised to deliver the Israelites from this plague if they would sacrifice a lamb and spread its blood on their doorposts. Then God would pass over their houses, because he would know that a lamb had been sacrificed as a substitute. And so, when God established his covenant with Israel, he commanded the people to celebrate their salvation from slavery and remember his covenant promises by celebrating the Passover meal.

Like Abraham, Israel was called for a purpose. In Exodus 19:6, God said that Israel was to be a "kingdom of priests." Think about what a priest does. He is supposed to talk to God for a group of people and talk to a group of people for God. If all the Israelites were supposed to be priests, this means they were supposed to represent God to the nations. Hundreds of years after God first gave them the law, he explained Israel's commission through the prophet Isaiah: "I will make you as a light for the nations, that my salvation may reach to the end of the earth" (Isa. 49:6).

As we read the story of the Old Testament, it becomes obvious that the Israelites failed in this mission. Instead of being a light to the nations, they became idolaters like the nations. And we saw earlier what came from that: exile in Babylon.

The New Covenant People of God

In the New Testament, God's covenant people are called the church. Now, before I get to the important part of what we need to say, I should mention something about the nature of the church. You see, a lot of Christians disagree about the relationship between Israel and the church. Some argue for a hard-and-fast line between Israel and the church (they are typically called dispensationalists). Other Christians might say that Israel and the church are just two ways of talking about the people of God (they are typically called covenant theologians).

Even though I'm more in the covenant theology camp myself, I've been in churches and schools with dispensationalists, and I'm thankful to say that this does not have to be a big dividing line between Christians. No matter what they think about the future of Israel, most Christians today recognize that the church gets to share in the promises to Israel. This is why Paul can say in Galatians 3:29, "If you are Christ's, then you are Abraham's offspring, heirs according to promise." Everyone who believes in Jesus is a part of the new covenant and gets to share in God's promises to Abraham and his family.

As he always has, God is calling his people into a community for the purpose of blessing the nations today. After his death and resurrection, Jesus gathered his disciples together and sent them out with a command to "make disciples of all nations" (Matt. 28:19). Like the old covenant people of God, they were marked out as a people to bless the nations. But in the new covenant age in which we live, God is actually working to accomplish this task. The fact that I'm a Gentile with Western European heritage and writing about Israel's God and Israel's Messiah is good evidence for this!

So we can't assume that our university campus group, neighborhood Bible study, or golfing foursome is the only Christian community we need. We need the church, because the church is God's covenant community today. Think of it this way: Jesus commanded us to gather in his name as the church (Matt. 18:15–20). This means that it does not make sense for people to say that they are followers of Jesus but that church isn't really their thing. That's like saying, "I'm a follower of Jesus, but following Jesus isn't my thing."

And even though Christians might disagree about some of the issues surrounding baptism and the Lord's Supper, we all can agree that God has given his new covenant community, the church, these two identifying marks. Just as circumcision was a way to identify who was a part of the old covenant, baptism is the way to identify members of the new covenant. Just as the celebration of the Passover was a way for God's covenant members to remember how God saved his people from slavery in Egypt, the Lord's Supper is the way for God's new covenant community to remember how he saved his people from their sin at the cross. Whether we call them ordinances, sacraments, or covenant signs, in the New Testament, Christians proclaim they are followers of Jesus by being baptized and declare their ongoing allegiance to Jesus by taking the Lord's Supper.

As the church fulfills its commission, taking the good news about Jesus to the nations, it is fulfilling the commission to extend God's saving reign to the nations. This is why Peter can say that we now are "a royal priesthood" (1 Pet. 2:9). And as more and more people submit to Jesus as Lord, more and more people enter his covenant community, the church. Because of this, Paul can conclude that the church is the particular place where God's glory is on display (Eph. 3:21). What other community would you rather be a part of?

Connecting Verses

Old Testament: Exodus 19:6
New Testament: 1 Peter 2:9

Summary Statement

To know the whole message of the Bible, we must know that from the beginning, God calls his people into a covenant community and blesses them so that they will bless the nations through Jesus, their covenant King.

9

LAND

Imagine it is the year 1900, and a young couple has a new baby boy. The man is full of Gilded Age optimism, so he tells his wife that he will work hard to build a successful business. And he promises that he will buy his son the best carriage on the market and the finest breed of horses to pull it when the boy grows up and gets married. As the years go by, the father's business prospers, and soon he has more than enough money to keep his promise. Finally, in 1925, the son announces that he is going to be married, so his father buys him a brand-new Ford Model T.

Did the father fail to keep his promise? After all, he bought his son a car, not a carriage. But this does not mean he broke his word. He promised his son the finest means of transportation available, and that is exactly what he gave him. The actual fulfillment of the promise was far greater than he could have imagined in 1900, so we cannot say that the father broke his promise.

I've heard several versions of this story from several teachers, but the point is always the same. Even though the nature of God's promises and their fulfillment is often beyond our greatest imaginings, their essential nature stays the same. It is especially important for us to understand this principle as we think about the Promised Land.

As we consider this theme, we first need to see the connection between the kingdom of God and the Promised Land. Even though God's kingdom is first his authority to reign, this does not mean God's kingdom isn't ultimately a place. God's kingdom will fill the new heaven and the new earth one day, and his people will live with him in that worldwide kingdom. This is a good example of how knowing the end helps us makes sense of the rest of the story. As we think about the Promised Land, we need to remember where the story is heading.

Inheritance

As you are reading through the Bible, you might notice an interesting shift when you move from the Old to the New Testament. In the Old Testament, God promises the Israelites a land and gives them that land, and even though they rebel against him and end up in Babylon, he brings them back to that land. Hundreds of times in the Old Testament, the word *inheritance* is used to refer to the land that God's people receive from him as a fulfillment of his covenant promises to Abraham.

But when we get to the New Testament, the language of "inheritance" takes a surprising backseat. The concept isn't used that often, but when it is, it seems different than it does in the Old Testament. For example, in Colossians 1:12, Paul says that we now "share in the inheritance of the saints in light." He explains what that means in the following verse: "He has delivered us from the domain of darkness and transferred us to the kingdom of his beloved Son" (v. 13). In other words, Paul says that the inheritance of God's people—which was the Promised Land in the Old Testament—now refers to our spiritual place in the kingdom of God.

Some people might read this and get a little nervous, saying that we are "spiritualizing" the land promises from the Old Testament. They might say, "You can't take a promise of a literal land, with trees and rocks and rivers, and say that it refers only to a spiritual reality." I absolutely agree. God will reign over his people in the land that he has promised to them. But that land is not simply a piece of real estate in the Middle East on the eastern edge of the Mediterranean Sea. It is much larger than that. And this expansion of God's promises helps us understand how Paul and the New Testament writers understand our inheritance and experience of the Promised Land right now. To see this, let's look at another place where Paul talks about the Promised Land.

Heir of the World

While he is unpacking the nature of saving faith in Romans 4, Paul says, almost in passing, that Abraham is the "heir of the world" (v. 13). You may have read this verse many times without stopping and thinking about what Paul is saying. In Genesis 15:18, God promised Abraham, "To your offspring I give this land, from the river of Egypt to the great river, the river Euphrates." Generally speaking, this is all of the land along the eastern coast of the Mediterranean. It is a big chunk of land—certainly larger than the modern borders of the nation of Israel. But Paul does not say that God promised Abraham the land on the eastern coast of the Mediterranean. He says that God promised him *the world* as his inheritance. How can he say this?

God promised to reign over his people and to live among

them in the place that he had promised to them. Once you understand the nature of God's kingdom and what the Bible teaches us about that kingdom, the nature of the Promised Land should click into focus fairly quickly. What does the trajectory of the Old Testament teach us about God's kingdom and presence? Among other things, we have seen that these promises point to the worldwide reign and presence of God. To see this, let's go back to the beginning of the story (again).

Back to the Beginning

Not only was the garden of Eden the first temple in the Bible, it was also the first "Promised Land." It was the place where God's people could live in perfect harmony with him and with the entire creation. It set the pattern. When sin and death entered the world, God cast Adam and Eve out of this perfect land. But the rest of the story of the Bible is God's glorious plan to bring his people into the land where they could again live in perfect harmony with him and the entire creation. Once God's people were evicted from the garden, they were looking for rest and a return to the Promised Land.

If we jump forward to Abraham, we can see that one of the fundamental covenant blessings that God gave to Abraham was the land. In Genesis 17, God said that "all the land of Canaan" would be Abraham's "everlasting possession" (v. 8). And we already saw that the borders of this land are "from the river of Egypt to the great river, the river Euphrates."

But God also promised to work through Abraham to bless the nations (Gen. 12:3). He told him he would have as many descendants as the sand on the beach or the stars in the sky (Gen. 15:5; 22:17). Next time you are at the beach, try to count the grains of sand. Or when you look into the clear night sky in the country, try to count the stars. It can't be done. And that is kind of the point—Abraham would have more descendants than we could count; more than we could imagine.

So on the one hand, God promised a specific tract of land to Abraham; on the other hand, he promised that he would have far more descendants than could ever fit into that land—in fact, in Genesis 17:5, God told Abraham that he would be the father of a multitude of *nations*. That alone should tip us off to the idea that while the Promised Land couldn't be less than what God said it would be, it sure could be a whole lot more.

As the rest of the Old Testament story unfolds, we see more hints about the way God would keep his land promises. After the exodus from Egypt (and forty years of wandering in the wilderness), the Israelites finally made it back to the Promised Land. It seemed like the promises to Abraham were fulfilled. In fact, Israel's victories in Canaan were so complete that the book of Joshua can say: "And the LORD gave them rest on every side just as he had sworn to their fathers. . . . Not one word of all the good promises that the LORD had made to the house of Israel had failed; all came to pass" (21:44–45). But as we continue to read through the Old Testament, we discover that there was still more to come.

After a bit of a bumpy road (if you want to know just how bumpy, read Judges), David eventually became king over Israel. The reigns of David and Solomon were the high point of Israel's power and influence in the Old Testament story. Like Joshua, David defeated the surrounding nations to conquer the land. Because of David's military victories, Solomon could say: "Blessed be the LORD who has given rest to his people Israel, according to all that he promised. Not one word has failed of all his good promise, which he spoke by Moses his servant"

(1 Kings 8:56). Sound familiar? Even though Joshua had already said these promises were fulfilled, during Solomon's reign, they were fulfilled again and in a greater way.

When King Solomon died, things in Israel went from bad to worse until God finally sent his people into exile. But there was still hope for God's people to receive the Promised Land. In fact, by the time of the prophecies of Isaiah, Israel was not just looking for the restoration of the Davidic monarchy in the land of Canaan. Instead, the people were looking for the reign of David's son over the entire creation. Isaiah 9:7 tells us that the coming Messiah will sit on the throne of David "from this time forth and forevermore." Along with this, Isaiah 65:17 tells us that God is creating a new heaven and a new earth as the place for the Messiah's eternal reign over the new creation. When God finally fulfills the promise of a land that he gave to Abraham so many years ago, there will be an eternal and universal kingdom, with plenty of room for all of those descendants of Abraham. Based on the Old Testament, then, I think Paul was right to say that Abraham was the heir of the world.

True Rest

When Paul talks about our inheritance in Christ, he is looking to the renewal of all things, when Christ will reign over the new creation. But as we live in the already and wait for the not yet, we experience our inheritance through the present spiritual reign of Christ. Since Christ is now reigning and advancing his kingdom as the gospel goes forward, it makes sense to see our inheritance as a present spiritual reality.

Hebrews also helps us understand the present spiritual experience of our inheritance. In both Joshua 21 and 1 Kings 8, the writers talk about God giving his people rest. This is a big part of the blessing of the Promised Land. Notice what the writer of Hebrews says about this rest. First, in Hebrews 4:8, he reminds us that Joshua did not give the Israelites the rest they ultimately sought. Sure, they experienced rest in some way, but there was a greater rest to come. Otherwise, why would Solomon have had to give the people rest? But the writer of Hebrews tell us that true rest comes through Jesus the Messiah, so that "we who have believed enter that rest" (Heb. 4:3). Even while we wait for the final inheritance, when God will make all things new, we can experience the rest that God promised to his people right now. We get to enjoy our inheritance right now. But there is more still to come.

One day, God will make all things new, and in the new creation that we see in Isaiah 65 and Revelation 21–22, we will finally enjoy rest in the Promised Land, where we will live in perfect harmony with God and the entire creation—a far better fulfillment than Abraham could have imagined. As we enjoy God's presence and his reign in that new creation, we will say in a greater way than Joshua, Solomon, or even the writer of Hebrews: "Blessed be the LORD who has given rest to his people Israel, according to all that he promised. Not one word has failed of all his good promise."

Connecting Verses
Old Testament: Joshua 21:44
New Testament: Hebrews 4:11

Summary Statement
To know the whole message of the Bible, we must know that the Promised Land points to the rest God's people experience now in Christ and ultimately in the new creation.

10

IDOLS

What comes to mind when you think about idols? Maybe you think of the opening scene from *Raiders of the Lost Ark*, when Indiana Jones carefully replaces a golden idol with a bag of sand (which doesn't turn out so well!). Your mind might go to ancient ruins in Greece or Rome and the temples built for gods such as Zeus, Poseidon, and Diana. Or maybe you've read the Bible enough to think of something like the golden calf that the Israelites made at Mount Sinai.

But I want us to think about idols by starting in the New Testament, in one of the last books in the Bible. Then we will come back to Mount Sinai and think about how idolatry fits into the story of the Bible.

Keep Yourselves from Idols

In 1 John, the apostle John is writing to remind Christians how they can be sure that they have life in Jesus the Messiah. After teaching the church about what it looks like to be united to Jesus and to love one another, John concludes with a comment that seems to come out of left field. In the last verse of his letter, he writes, "Little children, keep yourselves from idols" (1 John 5:21).

This is the first time John mentions idols in the whole letter. On top of this, the church in the New Testament did not struggle with the temptation to bow down to idols the way Israel did in the Old Testament. It is true that the apostle Paul mentions food offered to idols in his letters to the church at Corinth, but the issue there wasn't whether Christians should bow down and sacrifice to idols—it was whether they could eat food that had been offered to idols with clean consciences. Everyone agreed that idol worship was a no-no. So what exactly is John talking about?

While we can't know everything that might have been going on with the Christians to whom John was writing, he warns them many times in this letter about the dangers of having a wrong view of Jesus. Just a few verses earlier, he writes, "Whoever has the Son has life; whoever does not have the Son of God does not have life" (1 John 5:12). A right understanding of Jesus is essential for life in God's kingdom. John Stott is right to conclude, "All alternatives to the true God who has revealed himself in Jesus Christ, are properly 'idols' . . . from them the Christian must vigilantly guard himself."[11]

You see, idolatry might sound exotic, but it is a constant danger to the human heart, and it is one of the most damaging and damning sins that we see throughout the story of the Bible. David Foster Wallace was right to say: "There is no such thing as not worshipping. Everybody worships. The only choice we get is what to worship."[12] We are always looking for something to worship, and we are always in danger of idolatry because we want to create our own god to worship.

Did God Actually Say . . . ?

When the Serpent tempted Eve to disobey God by taking the fruit from the tree, he asked her, "Did God actually say . . . ?" (Gen. 3:1). When he convinced Eve to doubt and change what God had said, the Serpent distorted the reality of who God is. He also opened the door for Adam and Eve to want to be like God—to make an idol out of themselves. In that first temptation, Adam and Eve let the first seeds of idolatry into the world. And it did not take long for those seeds to flower.

Come with me next to the base of Mount Sinai. The exodus was one of those "new creation" moments we saw earlier. Just as they did after the first creation, God's people quickly fell into sin. Unlike the first creation, we don't see just a few hints of idolatry here. For many of us, what happened at Mount Sinai could be the very definition of idolatry.

After Moses had been on the mountain for forty days and nights, the Israelites began to doubt God's care for them. Like Adam and Eve, they decided to take matters into their own hands. They went to Aaron, Moses's brother, and asked him to make them a god they could worship. They were getting tired of having to worship someone they couldn't understand or control; they wanted a god that was a little more manageable.

After Aaron made the golden calf, the people said, "These are your gods, O Israel, who brought you up out of the land of Egypt!" (Ex. 32:4). Once again, they invented an alternative to the true God—and this time, in a tangible way. Even though Moses came down from the mountain and obliterated that golden calf, he could not obliterate the idolatry from the Israelites' hearts. It would take something far more drastic.

You Are What You Worship

The most important command in the law that God gave to Moses on Mount Sinai is really a warning against idolatry. Deuteronomy 6:4–5 teaches that Israel's God is the only true God. Because he is the only God, they were to love and worship him alone. But even though God sent many prophets to warn them, Israel continually failed to worship God exclusively.

From the time they entered the Promised Land, the Israelites kept chasing after other gods. In the years following David's kingdom, the constant test of whether the nation was faithful to God was whether the king led the people toward idols or away from them. More often than not, both the kings in Israel and the kings in Judah led the people further into idolatry. As you know by now, the result was judgment and exile.

God gives us one of the most vivid warnings against idolatry in the Bible in Psalm 115. After the psalmist describes the ridiculousness of idol worship (people put their trust in handmade images that can't do anything!), he gets to the really scary part in verse 8: "Those who make them become like them; so do all who trust in them." If you are going to worship an idol, expect to become like an idol. These idols were powerless, weak, and easily defeated by the powerful hand of the true God. Whoever worships such idols should expect the same.

I like the way Greg Beale summarizes the principle we see at work in Psalm 115: "What people revere, they resemble, either for ruin or for restoration."[13] This does not cut in just one direction. While it is true that if we worship idols, we will become powerless like them, it is also true that if we worship the true God, we will be made more and more into his image.

We can see both sides of this principle in Paul's letter to the Romans.[14] In Romans 1, we can see that the tendency of our hearts is to exchange the truth about God for a lie, worshiping and serving the creature rather than the Creator (v. 25). This is idolatry. But in these verses, idolatry does not take the form of bowing down to a carved image or a golden calf. It takes the form of asserting our own authority to determine who is in charge. It is really worshiping ourselves and our own desires, just as Adam and Israel did.

In the verses that follow, this worship is called "dishonorable passions" (v. 26). When we believe lies about God, it leads to misdirected passions—even to the point of worshiping our passions. It does not take much imagination to see the ways that this happens around us today. But as we worship those dishonorable passions, we become more and more dishonorable ourselves—as Paul puts it here, we are filled with all manner of unrighteousness. We become what we worship.

However, as Paul describes the solution to this idolatry in the following chapters of Romans, we discover that Jesus lived a perfect life and died the death that we idolaters deserve. As a result of this, "everyone who calls on the name of the Lord will be saved" (Rom. 10:13). And this salvation includes the reversal of what we see in Psalm 115.

Left to ourselves, we pursue and worship idols that ruin us. But in Christ, we turn away from our idolatry and worship the true and living God. When this happens to us, we no longer resemble idols, but we resemble this living God more and more. In fact, in Romans 8:29, Paul says that part of the great unbreakable chain of salvation is that those whom God calls he conforms to the image of his Son. As we worship him, we become like him.

John Calvin famously wrote that "man's nature, so to speak, is a perpetual factory of idols."[15] Throughout the Bible, the temptation to exchange the truth about God for a lie is an important and tragic theme. The people of God continually fell victim to idolatry. But through Christ, God finally broke the idolatrous chain that was wrapped around human hearts for thousands of years. Through Christ, we can overcome idolatry to serve the God we were made to worship. It is only because of Christ's work for us that we can keep ourselves from idols—whatever form they might take. When Christ returns to reign forever, the unbreakable chain of Romans 8 will continue—we will be fully conformed to the image of Jesus and glorified to live with him, worshiping and serving our God forever.

Connecting Verses

Old Testament: Leviticus 19:4
New Testament: 1 John 5:21

Summary Statement

To know the whole message of the Bible, we must know that though the temptation toward idolatry is a constant danger, through Christ, God keeps us from idols, and he will conform us completely to Christ's image.

11

JUDGMENT

I'm a big fan of classical Christian education. In fact, I just started working at a classical Christian school in Kailua, Hawai'i. Stop by and say hello if you are ever in town. I'm not trying to ride a hobbyhorse here, but I think there are a lot of benefits to this kind of education. One of these benefits is avoiding what C. S. Lewis called "chronological snobbery"—the belief that just because an idea is new, it is right (or because it is old, it is wrong).[16] We have a lot to learn from the wisdom of the past, and that is especially true as we think about biblical theology and the message of the Bible.

At our school, the students recite the Apostles' Creed regularly. If you don't know this creed, you should look it up and learn it well. It is one of the earliest summaries of the Christian faith outside of the Bible—it dates back to the second century after Christ (or maybe even earlier). Toward the end of the creed, we read these lines about Jesus: "He ascended to heaven and is seated at the right hand of God the Father almighty. From there he will come to judge the living and the dead."

Sometimes we forget that when Jesus returns, he will be returning for a purpose. Did you notice how the early Christians described this purpose? "To judge the living and the dead." At times, we think about Jesus's return like a science fiction story. We tend to overlook what the early Christians did not: Jesus is returning for judgment.

Now, you might be thinking, "This is going to be a bummer of a chapter; maybe I'll just move along to the next one." That is fine if you'd like. We are definitely going to look at some hard things. But if you hang with me, you might see something new and even glorious about how judgment moves the story of the Bible forward.

Salvation through Judgment

From the very beginning, our rebellion against God demanded judgment. When Adam and Eve failed to trust God and obey him, the immediate consequence was judgment. They were expelled from the garden and confronted with the cold, hard reality of life in a fallen world, a reality that ultimately ends in death. But even in judgment, there was hope that the Promised One would crush the head of the Serpent (Gen. 3:15). From the beginning, judgment and salvation were closely connected.

When we come to the story of Noah and the flood, we get another picture of the link between salvation and judgment. Because of their unrelenting sin and rebellion against him, God judged the human race with a flood that wiped them out—except for one family. Again, we might be tempted at this point to stop and think that God's judgment is rather harsh. Was it necessary for him to destroy the whole earth?

The short answer to this question is that God's justice demanded it. Every human being was flagrantly turning his or her back on God the Creator. Genesis tells us, "The LORD saw that the wickedness of man was great in the earth, and that every intention of the thoughts of his heart was only evil continually" (6:5). This great wickedness could not go unchecked. It had to be met with justice.

We don't have a problem talking about justice as long as it is not pointed at us. What do you do when you come to a traffic signal and have the right of way, but another driver cuts you off or speeds out in front of you? If you are like me, your hands go up in the air and you look around for a police officer to distribute swift and immediate justice. But what if you are on the expressway driving over the speed limit (not that you would ever do that), and you see that police officer you were looking for earlier. Are you looking for justice then—or mercy? We recognize the need for just judgment, but we don't want to be on the receiving end of it.

After God determined to judge the earth in the flood, he instructed Noah to build an ark to deliver him and his family from this judgment. Noah and his family "went into the ark to escape the waters of the flood" (Gen. 7:7). It was only because of the flood that Noah and his family could experience salvation. In fact, at least one scholar, Jim Hamilton, argues that "God's glory in salvation through judgment" is the central theme of the Bible.[17] While I wouldn't go quite that far, we can see that God's judgment is a key theme in both the story of the Bible and in the experience of salvation for God's people.

The Exodus

We can see the way God's judgment works again in the exodus from Egypt. In Exodus 6:6, God tells Moses, "I will redeem

[Israel] with an outstretched arm and with great acts of judgment." We will think more about redemption in the next chapter, but here we can see the connection between salvation and judgment: "I will redeem you . . . with great acts of judgment." Later, in Exodus 7:4, God says he will bring his people "out of the land of Egypt by great acts of judgment." In other words, God's judgment on Egypt would also be the way that he would save his people.

Once God delivered his people from Egypt, we get a closer look at the connection between God's judgment and his salvation. After the golden calf fiasco, Moses was back on the mountain, and he asked to see God's glory. But this was impossible. To look straight at the glory of God would have killed him. But God agreed to tuck Moses into a cleft in the rock and let him get the barest glimpse of the divine glory.

We don't know what Moses saw or felt when God's glory passed by, but I can promise you that the sight was far more intense than anything you've seen in a movie. However, we do get a little hint of what he heard. In Exodus 34:6–7, we are told that God passed by Moses and proclaimed, "The LORD, the LORD, a God merciful and gracious, slow to anger, and abounding in steadfast love and faithfulness, keeping steadfast love for thousands, forgiving iniquity and transgression and sin, but who will by no means clear the guilty, visiting the iniquity of the fathers on the children and the children's children, to the third and the fourth generation."

When Moses asked to see God's glory, he heard about two crucial aspects of God's nature. First, he is a God of salvation. He is merciful and gracious, keeping his covenant promises. But he is also a God of judgment and justice. He will by no means clear the guilty. He will judge sin and dole out the just penalty for everyone who keeps rebelling against him. He is a God who saves and who judges.

Throughout the Old Testament, both the mercy and justice of God are on display over and again. Through the sacrifices in the law, God's mercy and justice met. The deaths of the sacrificial animals reminded Israel that sin demanded a just payment. And they also reminded Israel that God was mercifully providing a means of escape. But those sacrifices were not sufficient to meet the ultimate demands of God's justice. There had to be a greater sacrifice.

The Cross

Have you ever considered that on the cross, Jesus was under the judgment of the Father? Our sin and rebellion against God deserve judgment—the same judgment that the flood brought, the same judgment that fell on Egypt, the same judgment that those Old Testament sacrifices embodied, and worse. But Jesus took our sin on his shoulders. Peter tells us, "He himself bore our sins in his body on the tree" (1 Pet. 2:24). Paul says, "For our sake he made him to be sin who knew no sin" (2 Cor. 5:21). On the cross, Jesus bore the judgment for sin that we deserve. Because of this, we are saved. Here, in the greatest salvation of all, God saved his people through judgment.

At the cross, we see both God's justice and mercy on display in a unique and glorious way. For God to be just, he must judge sin. But God also loves to abound in mercy. In the death and resurrection of Jesus, we see these two aspects of God's character come together. At the cross, God does not only judge sin. He does not only save his people. Instead, at the cross, God judges sin in order to save his people. His justice is the instrument that he uses to display his mercy!

God's Glory in Salvation and Judgment

In Exodus 33–34, Moses asked to see God's glory, and the Lord proclaimed himself to be a God of salvation and judgment. God showed Moses his glory by telling him how he saves his people by judging sin. As Hamilton says, God's glory is on display in salvation through judgment. While all things exist to give God glory, when we see both his mercy and his justice on display at the same time, God's glory is displayed in a special way.

Because of this, we should not be afraid to talk honestly about God's judgment. It is a theme that shows up again and again in the story of the Bible. But as we talk about God's judgment, we also cannot forget that when he judges sin, God is also at work to save his people. When Jesus returns to judge the living and dead, he will also save his people. And when he does this, he will put his glory on display for all the world to see.

Connecting Verses

Old Testament: Exodus 7:4
New Testament: 2 Corinthians 5:21

Summary Statement

To know the whole message of the Bible, we must see that God's glory is always on display when he judges sin and saves his people, and his glory shone brightest when Jesus took the judgment of sin on the cross to bring that salvation.

12

EXODUS

Even though I'm kind of a book nerd, I'm also a fairly big sports fan. Yes, a real renaissance man. Anyway, in my early high school years, I stayed up past midnight many nights during the college basketball season to watch the late games. Even if it was Santa Clara University against San Jose State, I'd stay up and watch it, just because I liked college basketball (no offense to fans of those schools). As the years have gone by and my responsibilities have piled up, I haven't been able to watch as many games as I'd like, but I still follow my Michigan teams closely. Go Blue!

Odds are that quite a few of you reading this book are sports fans as well. Americans spend somewhere around $500 billion every year on tickets, jerseys, and just about anything with a team's logo on it. Fans in other countries spend more than $1 trillion every year.

But it is not just what happens on the field of play that brings in those billions. It is the stories that surround the games—

especially stories of redemption. Think about it—everyone loves to see a down-and-out player or team turn it around to become a winner. Almost all professional sports leagues in the United States and many international leagues have some kind of "comeback player of the year" award, given to a player who overcomes adversity of some sort and redeems himself on the field.

One of the reasons that these redemption stories sell so well is that they reflect something everyone understands. We all know what it is like to be down and out, hurting, in a place we don't want to be. And we all know what it is like to long for deliverance from our hard circumstances, because we are all sinners in need of redemption, whether we realize it or not.

Although we've already pointed to it several times, in this chapter, we will look at how the exodus establishes a pattern for redemption in the rest of the Bible.

The Exodus

The first chapter of Exodus tells us that after the family of Abraham—about seventy people—went down to Egypt to escape a famine in the Promised Land, it eventually grew into a whole people group of hundreds of thousands. They really nailed the "be fruitful and multiply" command.

But just as Abraham's family was growing in number, a new royal family had come to power in Egypt. This Pharaoh did not remember how Abraham's great-grandson Joseph had helped Egypt during a famine. He saw the Hebrews, as Abraham's family was called, as nothing but a growing threat. What if they decided to try to revolt and take control? His was a new dynasty; he couldn't afford any threats to his power. So he enslaved the Hebrews. He forced them into backbreaking labor and ordered that their male children be killed. With no men, the race would eventually die out. His goal was to wipe the family of Abraham from the earth. When they cried out to God, Exodus 2:25 tells us, "God saw the people of Israel—and God knew." God knew his people whom he had chosen, he knew their pain, and he knew his promises to them. So he took action. This redemption story would put anything ESPN could produce to shame.

While Pharaoh was trying to wipe out all of the Israelite baby boys, one slipped through the cracks—or maybe we should say through the reeds! You see, one of the descendants of Abraham's great-grandson Levi had a baby boy, and he and his wife hid the baby from the king's executioners for three months. As the baby got bigger, they knew they could not hide him forever, so they put him in a basket in the reeds of the Nile River and prayed that God would save the boy's life.

Of all the people to find the baby, Pharaoh's own daughter "happened" upon the very spot along the river where the basket was floating. She took the baby, named him Moses, and raised him in her own house. And not only did she raise him herself, she also hired Moses's own mother as a nurse for him!

After Moses grew up, the story took an unexpected turn. Moses ended up killing an Egyptian who was beating one of his fellow Israelites, and he had to flee into the wilderness, where he spent the next forty years. Not exactly how he expected the story to turn out.

But God had promised to deliver his people even when their redemption seemed unlikely, and now he was going to use an unlikely leader to accomplish this redemption. As Moses was caring for his father-in-law's sheep in the wilderness, God appeared to him in the famous burning bush (Exodus 3). He told Moses that he is the great "I AM," the self-sufficient God. He does not need anything, but he supplies his people with everything. And this self-sufficient God keeps his promises. He would keep his promises to Abraham, Isaac, and Jacob by redeeming his people from their slavery in Egypt. Later, in Exodus 6:6, he put it like this: "Say therefore to the people of Israel, 'I am the LORD, and I will bring you out from under the burdens of the Egyptians, and I will deliver you from slavery to them, and I will redeem you with an outstretched arm and with great acts of judgment."

God promised to redeem his people. That was another way of saying that he would deliver them from their slavery to another master, Pharaoh, and bring them to the place where they could worship and serve him. And that is exactly what God did. Even though Pharaoh continued to resist him, God showed his power when he sent the ten plagues and when he saved Israel at the Red Sea. He brought the Israelites through the desert and provided for their needs along the way, even though their doubt led to them spending an extra forty years in the wilderness.

God had rescued his people, redeemed them from their slavery, and judged his enemies all in one mighty act. This pattern laid the foundation for understanding redemption in the rest of the Bible. When God works to redeem his people, he brings them out of bondage to another master so that they can serve him.

After they settled in the Promised Land, the Israelites continued to doubt and disobey him. For centuries, Israel struggled to remain faithful to God's covenant. After sending prophet after prophet to warn them, the Lord finally sent them into exile. Even before they were in the land, the Lord looked forward to the day when he would call his people back from their exile. In Isaiah 48:20–21, God calls to his people: "Go out from Babylon, flee from Chaldea, declare this with a shout of joy, proclaim it, send it out to the end of the earth; say, 'The LORD has redeemed his servant Jacob!' They did not thirst when he led them through the deserts; he made water flow for them from the rock; he split the rock and the water gushed out."

The New Exodus

When Israel returned from exile, God was building on the pattern of the exodus from Egypt. As you read the books of Ezra and Nehemiah and the prophecies of Haggai, Zechariah, and Malachi at the end of the Old Testament, you can see how God called his people out of Babylon and brought them back to the place where they could worship and serve him.

But there was a problem. The "new exodus" that the prophets tell us about was supposed to come with a new covenant (Jer. 31:31–34). Just as God established the law covenant after the first exodus, he promised a new covenant after the second exodus. This new covenant was supposed to change everything. But when the Jews returned to the Promised Land, things were not very different than before they left. Sure, they were back in the land, but they were still under the authority of the Persians (who had taken Babylon's place as the new superpower). Even though Israel had a brief period of independence in the second and first centuries BC, the Persians, then the Greeks, then the Romans were in charge. Even more important, the Israelites remained in slavery to sin. In the new covenant, God promised to remove their sin once and for all. But Israel continued to struggle with pride, strife, and many other sins.

Jesus's Exodus

So when we arrive at the New Testament, God's people are out of Babylon, but they are still in slavery to Rome and ultimately to sin. In other words, the second exodus was not yet finished.

When Joseph and Mary brought Jesus to the temple as a

baby, a prophetess named Anna was there, waiting for God to redeem his people—to finish the second exodus. When they brought in the baby, Luke tells us, "at that very hour she began to give thanks to God and to speak of him to all who were waiting for the redemption of Jerusalem" (Luke 2:38). She knew that Jesus would finish the redemption promised in the second exodus. When John the Baptist announced Jesus's coming in Mark 1:3, he did it by quoting Isaiah's prophecy of the second exodus: "Prepare the way of the Lord, make his paths straight" (see Isa. 40:3).

Later in Jesus's ministry, he took his three closest disciples, Peter, James, and John, with him to a mountain to pray. While Jesus prayed, his appearance changed so that they saw his glory in a remarkable way, and his clothes became bright white. Then Moses and the prophet Elijah appeared and talked with him about his upcoming death in Jerusalem. This scene is strange enough, but Luke uses an unusual word to refer to Jesus's death. Most English Bible versions translate it as "departure," but the Greek word actually means "exodus" (Luke 9:31).

Luke saw Jesus's death as the fulfillment of the new exodus that the prophets wrote about. How could Jesus do this? Well, the point of the first exodus was to redeem God's people from their slavery so that they could serve him. The new covenant came with the promise of a greater redemption—not just from Babylon or Persia, but from slavery to sin itself. To accomplish that redemption, Jesus "exodus-ed" in his death and resurrection to set God's people free from their slavery to sin.

Since he has finished this second exodus, Jesus is now redeeming God's people as they come to him in faith. In Revelation 18:4, God is calling to his people today: "Come out of her, my people, lest you take part in her sins, lest you share in her plagues." And as we see in Revelation 21, when this redemption is completed, God finally will bring his people into the Promised Land of the new creation.

Throughout the Bible, the exodus theme is a reminder that the God who began his work of redemption will see it through until the very end. The God of the first exodus is also the God who will finally bring his people home to the new creation. Talk about a great redemption story!

Connecting Verses

Old Testament: Exodus 6:6
New Testament: Luke 9:31 (be sure to read the text note!)

Summary Statement

To know the whole message of the Bible, we must know that when God works to redeem his people in both the exodus from Egypt and the second exodus that Jesus leads, he brings them out of their slavery so that they can serve him.

13

WISDOM

Do you like jigsaw puzzles? I like putting the last piece or two in a puzzle, but I'm not really patient enough to do the whole thing. But one of my sons is really good at puzzles. His mind just works that way. We have a video of him, made when he wasn't even two years old, putting together little puzzles faster than his older brother (or his parents!) could. No one else in our family has a mind quite like that—he just naturally knows how to fit the pieces together. He can do a five hundred-piece puzzle. I can't. If I try to do it, I end up jamming pieces into places where they don't really fit.

Fitting the different parts of the Bible into the whole story is kind of like doing a puzzle. When I teach about the story of the Bible, I sometimes remind people that knowing this story is like having the puzzle box with the picture on it. As we look at the individual pieces, we can glance back at the big picture and get a sense of how it all comes together.

For example, when we are reading Nehemiah, we can remember that Israel has returned from Babylon, but is still waiting for the new covenant promises. Or when we read Hebrews, we can remember that the Messiah has come and started fulfilling those new covenant promises. But what about when we read Proverbs or Ecclesiastes? How do those books fit into the story of the Bible?

To be honest, some people say that these books *don't* fit. They might say that trying to wedge them into the story of the Bible is like trying to fit pieces into a puzzle where they don't belong. But I don't think that is a good analogy. When I try to stick pieces in the wrong places, the problem is not that they aren't part of the puzzle. The problem is that I'm just not patient enough to figure out their proper places in the puzzle. And I think this is often true of us when we are dealing with books such as Proverbs. We aren't patient enough to think of them in light of the whole message of the Bible.

The Fear of the Lord Is the Beginning of Wisdom

We often refer to Proverbs, along with the books near it (Job, Ecclesiastes, and Song of Solomon) as Wisdom Literature. Of course, these books are not the only places where we find wisdom in the Bible. We see examples of wise men and wise sayings throughout the Scriptures. But these books—especially Proverbs—are a helpful starting place for us to understand the wisdom theme in the story of the Bible.

At times, it is easy to forget that Proverbs is not just a book full of helpful tips for a happy life. It is so intensely practical that we don't see that Proverbs is set in the same context as the rest of the Old Testament—it is part of the revelation of God to his covenant people, Israel. In other words, Proverbs is embedded in Israel's history. So we need to think about who wrote these proverbs and why they were written.

We can find the answer to both of these questions in the first few verses in Proverbs. First, Proverbs 1:1 tells us that Solomon, King David's son, wrote most of the Proverbs. He probably wrote both Ecclesiastes and Song of Solomon as well. Even though we know that Solomon was not the Promised One who would reign forever, the great things that Solomon accomplished were somewhat like a down payment, or reminder, that God keeps his promises. God used the wisdom he gave to Solomon to expand David's kingdom, at least for a generation.

This historical context reminds us that Wisdom Literature does not exist in a vacuum. It is part of the larger story of the Bible. The king of Israel, the heir to David's throne, was the primary model and teacher of wisdom for God's people. This is an important part of the overall story of the Bible.

And that leads us to the second question—why were the Proverbs written? To answer this, we need to read only a few more verses into the book. In Proverbs 1:7, Solomon writes, "The fear of the LORD is the beginning of knowledge; fools despise wisdom and instruction." Think about what is going on here. The king of Israel, the heir of King David, who was the ancestor of King Jesus, is telling us that the foundation for knowledge and wisdom is to fear and honor the Lord, the covenant God of Israel. This kind of wisdom points us to the overall message of the Bible as a book about God and his glory.

But these are not the only connections between wisdom and the story of the Bible. Later in Proverbs, wisdom is closely linked to God's work in creation itself. For example, Proverbs 8:23 tells us that wisdom was with God "at the first, before the beginning of the earth." In some way, wisdom was present with God as he created the mountains, the skies, and the seas. In a manner of speaking, wisdom guided or shaped the creation itself.

This makes sense if we think about the way wisdom works in the rest of Proverbs. The proverbs often teach us what it looks like for things to work as God intended them to work. In other words, they are talking about bringing order out of chaos. Whether it is the character of the wise contrasted with the character of a fool (see, for example, Prov. 10:1) or different aspects of the character of the righteous (see, for example, Prov. 10:20–25), Proverbs teaches us how we ought to live in a way that fits with God's creation design.

In the Old Testament, the king of Israel is the teacher of wisdom. Also, wisdom can never be separated from fear of the Lord. In other words, a truly wise person fears and trusts Israel's God, the only true God. Finally, wisdom helps us know how best to live in the world that God created for us. All three of these pieces fit nicely into the message of the Bible that we have been weaving throughout this book—and that message culminates with Jesus himself.

The Wisdom of Jesus

When you turn to the New Testament and start reading Jesus's teaching in the Gospels, a lot of what he says sounds like Proverbs and other Wisdom Literature. Jesus's most famous sermon, the Sermon on the Mount, begins and ends with wisdom themes. The Beatitudes at the beginning of the sermon sound suspiciously like Proverbs. He describes the "blessed" life as a life of wisdom. At the end of the sermon, Jesus compares the wise to the foolish—you may remember that the wise man builds his house on the rock and the foolish man builds his house on the sand (Matt. 7:24–27). In several other places, Jesus uses riddles and parables—just like we often find in the wisdom writings of the Old Testament. When we know the whole message of the Bible, this is what we should expect. The King of Israel, the Son of David, is a teacher of wisdom. As Jesus himself says later, when he is present, someone greater than Solomon is there (Matt. 12:42).

Since Jesus, the King of Israel, teaches us what a wise life looks like, fearing the Lord is also an important part of his message. In Matthew 10:28, he says that we shouldn't fear the one who can kill the body, but the one who can cast our bodies and souls into hell. In other words, we must fear the Lord. Again, when we know the story of the Bible, we expect to see Israel's King teaching that Israel's God ought to be feared and honored. This is at the heart of wisdom, and it is also at the heart of Jesus's teaching.

As we think about the third theme we saw in Proverbs, we don't have to go far in the New Testament to see the connections between Jesus and creation. In John 1, Jesus is identified as the Word, God himself, through whom all things were made. Some scholars argue that since wisdom is depicted in Proverbs 8 almost acting like a person, Jesus should be seen as kind of an embodiment of wisdom. This could be true, but I think it fits better with John 1 to see Jesus as the wise Creator himself.

But Jesus is not only the Lord of the first creation. He is also the Lord of the new creation. In Proverbs, wisdom teaches us how God created the world to function. Another way to think about wisdom's contribution to creation is to understand that it helps bring order out of chaos. Since the greatest chaos in this fallen world is sin and all that results from it, we should expect the greater wisdom to resolve the chaos of sin. This is exactly what we find in the greatest wisdom of all, the wisdom of the cross.

The Wisdom of the Cross

During the life of the apostle Paul, the church in Corinth was rather impressed by the wisdom of Greco-Roman philosophers. The Corinthian believers may have even thought of themselves as wise people, because they understood what makes the world go around. But the problem with most Greco-Roman wisdom was that it focused on the eloquence and rhetoric of the teacher—not on God's created order or his plan to overcome the chaos of sin.

When Paul wrote to the Corinthians, he turned the so-called wisdom of the world on its head. He told them that Jesus the Messiah is the power and the wisdom of God (1 Cor. 1:24). The wisdom of the cross is that God humbles people who think they are something and exalts those who know they are nothing. If God means for wisdom to teach us his design for the world, then the greatest wisdom of all is God's wisdom on display through Jesus. It is through Jesus that God has accomplished his purpose for the world, because it is through the cross that God is restoring order in the new creation.

There is a lot more to be said about Wisdom Literature in the Bible, but we at least can say this much: the king—that is, the King, Jesus the Messiah—teaches us that wisdom is about the God of Israel, the God who created all things. And the goal of all wisdom is the renewal of God's created order. Where else is this on display more than in the cross? When we are reading the wisdom writings, let's make sure we are connecting them to the whole story of the Bible in this way.

Connecting Verses

Old Testament: Proverbs 1:7
New Testament: 1 Corinthians 1:24

Summary Statement

To know the whole message of the Bible, we must know that Jesus the Messiah is the wise teacher who points us to the Creator God and reminds us that the goal of wisdom, the renewal of the creation order, was accomplished at the cross.

14

LAW

Go ahead and admit it: the Old Testament law can be confusing. At times, it's difficult to understand, and it can be hard to know what does or does not apply to us today.

You might have thought about this if you've read Leviticus 19 recently. In verse 18 of this chapter, God commands Israel, "You shall not take vengeance or bear a grudge against the sons of your own people, but you shall love your neighbor as yourself." But in the very next verse, he also tells them, "You shall not sow your field with two kinds of seed, nor shall you wear a garment of cloth made of two kinds of material" (v. 19).

We certainly ought to love our neighbors. But are we also supposed to worry about wearing clothes with two kinds of material? How can we know which commands apply to Christians? This confusion leads many people to accuse Christians of picking and choosing which laws to keep and not to keep.

At first glance, even some parts of the New Testament seem as if they don't help us understand the law any better. In the

Sermon on the Mount, Jesus says, "Do not think that I have come to abolish the Law or the Prophets" (Matt. 5:17). But then Paul says: "Circumcision is nothing and uncircumcision is nothing. Keeping God's commands is what counts" (1 Cor. 7:19 NIV). Isn't circumcision one of the commands of God in the law?

How then should we think about the law? Does all of it apply today? Only part of it? None of it? These are not simple questions, but I think one reason why many Christians fail to understand the law is that they don't understand the role it plays in the story of the Bible.

The Torah

Most of the time, when New Testament writers use the word *law*, they are talking about the covenant God made with Israel at Mount Sinai. So that is how we are going to use it in this chapter. We also need to be careful not to confuse a modern legal code with the Old Testament law. The word translated as "law" in the Old Testament is the Hebrew word *torah*. You may have heard the first five books of the Bible called the Torah—that is just another way of calling them the law. While the Torah does teach us what was legal and illegal in Israel, it has a fuller meaning than what you or I might mean by *Law*. In the Old Testament, *torah* means something like "instruction" or "teaching." If God designed the Torah to teach Israel something, what was it supposed to teach?

To answer that question, we have to remember where the law fits into the story of the Bible. Remember, God's covenant with Israel was built on his previous covenant with Abraham. God promised to give Abraham many descendants, to give him the Promised Land, and to bless all of the nations through him. We see connections to all three of these promises at work when God led the Israelites out of Egypt and gave them the law.

First, during their four hundred-year stay in Egypt, the family of Abraham grew into a full-fledged nation, just as God had promised Abraham. In addition, most of the law was focused on how Israel was to live in the Promised Land. Several times, while instructing the people about how to live under his covenant, God said things like, "When you come into the land of Canaan . . . ," followed by some specific teaching. Finally, just like the covenant with Abraham, the law was not supposed to be an end in itself. God told the people of Israel that they were to be a kingdom of priests (Ex. 19:6). This meant that as his chosen people, they were to represent God to the nations and even bless the nations. Again, we can see that the law was built on and was even the means by which God kept his promises to Abraham.

As we think about all of the commandments of the law covenant, we have to keep this connection to the covenant with Abraham in mind. God set Israel apart from the nations, but not to be a hermit people. Instead, he set Israel apart to be a light to the nations. The law itself points beyond its intentions for Israel. In the same way, the sacrifices of the law were not an end in themselves. Instead, like the law itself, they were designed to point to God's greater promises.

So we cannot assume the law was designed as a terrible burden, as a way to punish Israel, or, worst of all, as the way for people to earn God's favor in the Old Testament (with grace being something new in the New Testament). After all, before God gave Israel the Ten Commandments, he reminded them of what he had already done for them—he had graciously brought them out of slavery in Egypt (Ex. 20:2).

We also have to recognize that it is one thing to receive a gift, but it is another thing to be able to handle that gift. A few years back, *Extreme Makeover: Home Edition* was a hit TV show. Every week, the crew would show up at a needy family's house and send them off on a lavish vacation while they remodeled and improved their house. The family would come back in a week to what was essentially a brand-new house. The show would then fade out with the family enjoying their new pool in their remodeled backyard. But once the TV cameras left, families were often left with massive property tax and utility bills on their upgraded properties. The problem was, the producers of the show did not always consider whether the families would be able to handle the gifts they were being given; in many cases, they found out too late that they couldn't.

This is similar to what the law covenant was like for Israel. It was an amazing gift that came with unique responsibilities. But unlike the producers of *Extreme Makeover*, God knew that Israel would not be able to handle this gift apart from his gracious help. As we've already seen, the Israelites failed to keep the law covenant. They did not keep the laws that set them apart from the nations, they did not offer the sacrifices that would point to a great sacrifice to come, and they did not serve as priests representing God to the nations. They could not keep the law, and the result was a curse (Deut. 28:15). And Israel's failure to keep the law teaches us about the need for someone who can keep it.

Jesus and the Law

The connection between the law covenant and the covenant with Abraham is also important to keep in mind as we think about Jesus and the law. When Jesus taught about the law, he did not simply throw it out as an outdated, unenlightened moral code. After all, he said, "Do not think that I have come to abolish the Law" (Matt. 5:17). Jesus recognized the divine authority of the law. But he continued in the same verse, "I have not come to abolish [it] but to fulfill [it]."

What then does it mean to say that Jesus fulfilled the law? We have to start by seeing that Jesus perfectly obeyed it. He kept the covenant when Israel could not. Later in the New Testament, Hebrews teaches us that, unlike all other priests—who, under the law, had to offer sacrifices for their own sins—Jesus is without sin (Heb. 4:15). He was the only one to keep the law covenant perfectly. Because of this, Hebrews 7:27 tells us, he could offer himself as a perfect sacrifice to pay the price for the sins of God's people.

As we think about the law today, we have to see it as a fulfilled covenant. Jesus did what Israel could not do—he kept the law perfectly. He kept its stipulations, he was the faithful covenant partner, and he was the priest to the nations that Israel could not be. Because he kept it and fulfilled it, the law as a covenant no longer applies to us. Provisions such as the prohibition against wearing clothes with mixed fabrics were a unique part of the law covenant that set Israel apart from the nations. Jesus's obedience made these parts of the law obsolete. They belong to a fulfilled covenant. To say otherwise would be to deny Jesus his rightful place as the one who fulfilled the law.

But can we and should we keep some aspect of the law covenant today? If so, how? To answer this question, let's briefly turn to Paul's letters.

Paul and the Law

Through the centuries, hundreds of books have been written about Paul's view of the law, so keep in mind that there is a lot more to this discussion than we can cover here. But one of the most important passages for understanding Paul's view of the law is Romans 8:3–4. Paul says that through Jesus, God "condemned sin in the flesh, in order that the righteous requirement of the law might be fulfilled in us." Because Jesus condemned sin in the flesh—that is to say, he succeeded where Israel failed in keeping the commandments and in completing the sacrifices of the law, as we saw above—we are now able to keep the heart of the law: to love God and love our neighbors.

Remember how we explained covenants in chapter 4? They require both God and the human partner to fulfill their obligations. Even though Israel could not do it, Jesus fulfilled the obligations of the law covenant. Because of that, he established a new covenant as a way to keep the promises of the law covenant.

Because the new covenant builds on and advances the main purpose of the law covenant, Paul still sees a place for the prophecies from the law and the wisdom of the law for Christians.[18] But now the law of Christ in the new covenant, not the law covenant, guides our obedience to God (1 Cor. 9:21). We keep the intent of the law by keeping the commands of Christ as members of the new covenant.

The Law and the Christian

Run, John, run,
The law commands,
But gives me neither feet nor hands.
Far better news
The gospel brings.
It bids me fly and gives me wings.

This little poem is usually attributed to John Bunyan, the author of *The Pilgrim's Progress*. No matter who actually wrote it, it expresses an important truth for understanding the role of the law covenant in the Old Testament. It is like those houses on *Extreme Makeover*. Sure, it is a gracious gift, but if the recipient lacks the ability to make the tax and utility payments, its purpose cannot be fulfilled. But when Christ came to fulfill the law, he made all of the payments we will ever owe. And now we can fulfill the purpose of the law covenant, which is ultimately rooted in the covenant with Abraham. We can love God and proclaim his glory as a way of loving and blessing the nations.

When Paul says that circumcision does not matter, he means that the people of God do not need to be circumcised to be faithful to God's covenant any longer. What really counts in the new covenant is whether we keep the commands of God in Christ. While we still struggle against sin, because Christ has won the decisive victory, we can struggle with confidence, and know that through the power of the gospel and the gift of the Holy Spirit, we really can keep God's commands. In our next chapter, we will think a little more about this new covenant gift of the Spirit.

Connecting Verses

Old Testament: Deuteronomy 28:15
New Testament: Romans 8:3–4

Summary Statement

To know the whole message of the Bible, we must know that although Israel failed to keep the law, Jesus fulfilled the law in his perfect life and sacrificial death, so that we are now able to keep the heart of the law as new covenant Christians.

15

SPIRIT

The boys in my house are big *Star Wars* fans (yes, including me). We love the *Star Wars* movies, old and new, and if you come to our house for dinner, you might get recruited into a Jedi battle.

But I should be clear that our love for *Star Wars* doesn't mean we are exactly cool with the worldview on display in the movies. Even though I'd say there is still an essential battle between good and evil, some of the non-Christian religious influences make the movies a little confusing at times—especially when the characters talk about the Force. In the *Star Wars* universe, the Force is a kind of mystical power that somehow binds the universe together—and helps Luke Skywalker do cool stuff like lifting a boulder with his mind.

I don't think the Force is a serious threat to biblical Christianity, but I do think many people tend to confuse the Holy Spirit with the Force. In fact, in a 2014 survey, 63 percent of respondents admitted that they think the Holy Spirit is more like a force than a person.[19]

I can understand why people tend to think this way, especially if they aren't familiar with the story of the Bible. In our minds, the word *spirit* can be somewhat vague. We talk about "the spirit of the age" or say that an athlete has a "fighting spirit." But when we dig into the story of the Bible, we see that the Holy Spirit is an active divine person, fully engaged in the mission of God in the world.

The Holy Spirit at Creation

Did you know that the Father, the Son, and the Holy Spirit were all involved in the creation of the world? In 1 Corinthians 8:6, Paul says that all things are from the Father. In John 1:3, we learn that the Word, Jesus the Messiah, is the one through whom all things were created.

But in Genesis 1, we also get a big hint at the Holy Spirit's role in creation. After the first moment of creation, the world was formless and void. But "the Spirit of God was hovering over the face of the waters" (v. 2). Then God spoke the rest of creation into being and order. While Genesis does not tell us exactly what role he played, the Holy Spirit was clearly active at the very beginning, accomplishing the Father's purposes and bringing order out of chaos during that creation week. But his work did not stop there. Once sin entered the world, the Holy Spirit was also closely involved in the work of restoration and new creation.

The Holy Spirit in the Leaders of Israel

It's OK to admit that it can be challenging to understand how the Spirit was at work in the Old Testament. But if we remember that the Spirit was fully engaged in the mission of God and working to accomplish that mission, we should be able to track the work of the Spirit fairly closely as we watch God's redemptive plan unfold in the Bible.

We've already seen that Israel's exodus from Egypt was a central part of God's work of redemption in the Old Testament. To help them as they led God's people, the Spirit was "on" Moses first (Num. 11:17) and later on his successor, Joshua (Num. 27:18). What did it mean for the Spirit to rest on Moses or Joshua? To put it simply, it probably meant that the Spirit was giving these men exactly what was necessary to lead God's people as they came out of Egypt and into the Promised Land. He was giving them the help, wisdom, and strength they needed as God kept his covenant promises through them.

During the days of Israel's kings, we see something similar happening. Though the Spirit was given first to King Saul, it is especially important to see the Spirit's ministry in the life of King David. When Samuel anointed David as king, "the Spirit of the LORD rushed upon David" (1 Sam. 16:13). When this happened, the presence and power of the Holy Spirit was with David for the rest of his life.

After his greatest sin, when he committed adultery with Bathsheba and had her husband, Uriah, killed, David pleaded for God's forgiveness and asked that God would not take the Holy Spirit from him (Ps. 51:11). David turned away from his sin and threw himself on God's mercy. That is exactly what God gave him: mercy.

Even though David and his sons kept sinning, God promised that one day the greatest Son of David, the Messiah, would have the Spirit of the Lord resting on him (Isa. 11:2). In the culmination of God's saving plan, the Holy Spirit would play a vital role in the life of the Messiah, just as he always gave the leaders of

God's people power, help, and direction to accomplish God's mission in the plan of redemption.

The Holy Spirit and the Prophets

When we started looking at the work of the Holy Spirit in the Old Testament, you might have expected us to turn to the prophets first. After all, the Spirit shows up more times in the writings of the prophets than in any other section of the Old Testament, and the ministry of the Old Testament prophets was self-evidently and directly dependent on the Holy Spirit.

Unlike his work among the leaders of Israel, the Spirit did not rest on those prophets permanently. Instead, the Spirit would tell the prophets how God was at work, and they would communicate that message to God's people. This is basically what we see the prophets doing throughout the Old Testament—communicating what God wanted his people to hear. This helps us see why the judgment of God is so severe—because Israel would not listen to the very words of the Lord that came through his prophets (Zech. 7:12).

In the Old Testament, the Spirit worked in specific ways for specific people to do specific things. Not all of God's covenant people in the Old Testament experienced the Holy Spirit in these ways. In fact, when the Spirit was resting on Moses, he said that he wished all of God's people shared his experience of the Spirit (Num. 11:29). Near the end of the Old Testament, this is exactly what God said would happen. In Joel 2, God promised that when the new covenant was established, he would pour out his Spirit on all of his people (v. 28). And in the New Testament, we see the Spirit being poured out—first in the life of Jesus, and then on everyone who has faith in Jesus.

Jesus and the Holy Spirit

Have you ever noticed that in every part of Jesus's ministry, he was dependent on the Holy Spirit? That might surprise you, especially when you remember who Jesus is. In the first chapter of John's Gospel, we can read about how Jesus, the Word, God himself, was responsible for the creation of all things, yet he came to live among his people. Even though he is God, who made all things, he humbled himself to become a man who was always dependent on the Holy Spirit.

In Mark's Gospel, we read that the Holy Spirit led Jesus into the wilderness, where the Devil tempted him. And this wasn't just a gentle, passive leading. Mark tells us that the Spirit "drove him out into the wilderness" (1:12). The Holy Spirit was directly and powerfully involved in Jesus's ministry from the very beginning. Also, both Matthew and Peter tell us that Jesus was empowered by the Holy Spirit. Jesus himself told the Pharisees that he was casting out demons by the Spirit of God (Matt. 12:28). Later, as Peter was telling the good news to the first Gentile who believed in Jesus, Cornelius, he said that "God anointed Jesus of Nazareth with the Holy Spirit and with power" (Acts 10:38). The Spirit's help was crucial in Jesus's ministry. The Holy Spirit was even directly responsible for Jesus's resurrection (Rom. 8:11). And not only did the Spirit empower every part of Jesus's life, but he also gives life and power to all who are trusting him as well.

The Spirit and the Mission of the Church

After Jesus rose from the dead, his followers were confused and scared. We can't really blame them. They had spent years following Jesus, not always understanding what he was up to, but always sure that he knew what he was doing. But he was executed on the cross, and their worlds were turned upside down. Then, three days later, he rose from the dead and appeared to his followers again. After he rose, Jesus told his disciples to wait for the day when they would be "clothed with power from on high" (Luke 24:49).

About forty days later, that is exactly what happened. Jews from all over the Roman Empire had gathered in Jerusalem to celebrate the day of Pentecost, which is kind of like the anniversary of when God gave Israel the law. But this day, they got an even greater gift than the law. Finally, Moses's prayer from Numbers 11 was answered and Joel's prophecy began to be fulfilled. The Holy Spirit gave power to the apostles first and then to the rest of God's people, and they began to proclaim the good news.

In the rest of the book of Acts, we see the Spirit at work. He gives the church power and help to fulfill her mission. Whatever else we might want to say about "spiritual gifts," we have to recognize that they are called that for a reason. They are gifts— we can't brag about them because we don't really have anything to do with getting them. And they are "spiritual." They come only through the work of the Holy Spirit. Even now, the Spirit is giving power to every follower of Jesus to be a part of his mission. We are living in the age of fulfillment, waiting for Jesus to return to wrap it all up. But in the meantime, we can lean on the power of the Spirit.

In Romans 8:12–30, Paul gives us a little window into what the Holy Spirit does for the Christian today. If you are wondering how the Spirit is involved in your life, take a few minutes to read that passage and look at all the things he does. He gives us power to put sin to death (v. 13). He leads us (v. 14). He gives us confidence that we are children of God (v. 16). He helps us in our weakness (v. 26). He intercedes for us (v. 27). He does all of this so that we might grow in Christlikeness and proclaim his glory to those around us.

Finally, as you read through Revelation 3–4, you'll notice that the apostle John writes several times that the Spirit is speaking to the churches. At the end of the book, he says that the Spirit and the Bride are inviting us to come and drink from the water of God's Word. The point John is making is that the Spirit now helps us understand and apply God's Word so that we can know the God of the Bible and join him in the mission of calling the thirsty to "take the water of life without price" (Rev. 22:17). And so, in our last chapter, we want to consider this mission and our place in it.

Connecting Verses

Old Testament: Numbers 11:29
New Testament: Acts 2:17

Summary Statement

To know the whole message of the Bible, we must know that the Holy Spirit has been at work since the creation of the world—empowering God's redemptive plan, strengthening Jesus to carry out his work, and equipping the church to fulfill the mission of Jesus.

16

MISSION

Do you have a personal mission statement? If you don't, it is not a bad idea to create one. It can help you stay grounded in the things that are most important to you and that you feel God has called you to accomplish. This is why institutions have mission statements. Without a clear and defined mission, a business, a school, or even a church can easily wander away from its central purpose and waste a lot of time.

Do you think the Bible has a mission statement? Well, we've seen already that the purpose of the new covenant was actually to fulfill the promises of the covenant with David and the law covenant. But remember that the purpose of those covenants was to fulfill the covenant with Abraham. And the covenant with Abraham can really be traced all the way back to the first covenant and God's commitment to his creation. We could even say that all of these covenants are accomplishing some kind of mission. And we could say that whatever God intends to accomplish with these covenants is the central mission of the Bible.

So what are all these covenants intended to do? We've seen the answer in part in other chapters, but in this last chapter, we are going to pull together some of the remaining strands that point us toward the mission of God that unfolds for us in the Bible.

Among All the Nations

Luke 24 is one of my favorite chapters in the Bible, because it is a little window to the confusion, excitement, and glory of the day Jesus rose from the dead. While Jesus appeared to several others throughout the day, there is something unique about his appearance on the road to Emmaus, which is recorded in this chapter. This is partly because we not only see the risen Messiah, but we also get to hear a little bit of his teaching.

To set the scene, two of Jesus's followers were walking from Jerusalem to a small village called Emmaus, about seven miles away. As they were walking and talking along the way, Jesus joined them, but they did not recognize him. While the three of them walked together, these disciples told Jesus about all the things that had happened recently, including the shocking and tragic end to Jesus's life. Then Jesus responded in a surprising way. He told them that they should have seen this coming—and he walked them through the Old Testament, from Moses to the Prophets, teaching them "in all the Scriptures the things concerning himself" (Luke 24:27). When they arrived in Emmaus, Jesus finally revealed himself to them, but then he somehow disappeared (don't ask me how). The two disciples did not quite know what to do, but they knew they couldn't keep quiet about this. So they ran seven miles back to Jerusalem in the dark.

As the two disciples from Emmaus were telling everyone

what had happened, Jesus somehow appeared in the room. Again he taught about himself from the Old Testament. Remember, that was the only Bible the disciples had at that point. In Luke 24:46–47, we read that he told them three things that the Old Testament teaches about the Messiah. First, he had to suffer. He had done this once and for all on the cross. Second, he had to rise from the dead on the third day. He had done this on that first Easter Sunday. But the third thing was not something that would happen right away. He told them that "repentance for the forgiveness of sins . . . in his name" must be proclaimed to all the nations (Luke 24:47). The cross and resurrection were one-time events. But the proclamation of Jesus to the nations continues until the very moment you are reading this book and beyond.

The Mission of God in the Old Testament

God has intended to bless the nations through the family of Abraham from the beginning. Part of Israel's failure was its inability to do that. But even after centuries of failure, Israel's prophets kept pointing forward to the purposes of God beyond Israel. Even when they were talking about God redeeming Israel, the prophets said that when this happened, the nations would be blessed as well. You may not have noticed it before, but this is an important theme in Isaiah's prophecies.

When the prophet Isaiah began to declare God's message, God's people were in a tough spot. The nation had split into two, and the northern kingdom, Israel, was on the verge of being annihilated by the Assyrians, who also were a serious threat to the southern kingdom, Judah. On top of this, the king who had reigned in Judah for over fifty years had just died.

Even though Israel was hanging by just a thread, Isaiah kept reminding the people that God's plan was to bless the nations. Early in Isaiah's ministry, God gave him a vision of the nations coming to the house of the Lord to follow him (Isa. 2:2). Then, at the end of Isaiah's prophecy, God said that the "coastlands far away, that have not heard my fame or seen my glory," would hear of his glory (66:19). If you are new to the Bible, when you see a theme repeated at both the beginning and the end of a book or section, then you know it is fairly important. So God's mission to bless the nations was a significant part of Isaiah's message.

Think of how that would have sounded in Israel and Judah. "Sure, the most powerful nations on earth are about to pummel you, but don't forget that your call is to bless those nations." Talk about learning to love your neighbors. Israel's mission was to be the vessel that God would use to bless the nations. And even though the Israelites failed to do this, Jesus fulfills and finishes all that the people of God were promised to have and intended to be.

The Mission of God in the New Testament

In Luke 24, Jesus was preparing his disciples to continue the mission of God's people from the beginning—they were going to be the ones who took the gospel to the nations. But they weren't ready just yet. They had to wait about forty days.

In Luke's sequel to his Gospel, Acts, we read about what happened on the day of Pentecost, when the Holy Spirit fell on those disciples in an amazing way. Within a few weeks, thousands of Jewish people who had previously rejected Jesus had put their faith in him. But this explosive outreach did not stop in Jerusalem or in Judea. The message of the gospel continued to advance through the whole Roman Empire. In Acts, we watch the gospel spread to the Gentiles through Peter and then Paul. Paul kept taking the good news about Jesus farther and farther west toward Rome, the capital of the world in the minds of the first Christians. Within about twenty years or so, Paul could write that the gospel had spread from Jerusalem all the way around the Mediterranean Sea to Illyricum, which is near modern-day Croatia, across the Adriatic Sea from Italy (see Rom. 15:19). And these were the days before email, texting, or even printed pages.

But the mission of God's people did not end at Rome; or at the western end of the Mediterranean Sea in Spain; or in Europe, Asia, or North America. You see, just before Jesus ascended to heaven to return to his Father, he had given his followers a commission (Matt. 28:18–20). Most Christians call it "the Great Commission."

This was the last thing Jesus told his disciples before returning to heaven, so we need to pay careful attention to it. He told them to make disciples of people from every nation, baptizing them into God's people as a sign that they were a part of his covenant. In other words, Jesus commanded his followers to continue his fulfillment of the covenant with Abraham. Through the true son of Abraham, they were to take the blessing of Abraham to the nations.

Some Christians through the centuries have lost sight of this central theme in the Bible. Though not many say this now, some Christians have even argued that the Great Commission was only for that first generation of disciples. Once the gospel made it to Rome, they said, the commission was fulfilled. In fact, this is the argument some Christians made against William Carey when he set out to prepare to be a missionary in the late 1700s. In a meeting of Baptist pastors in England, when Carey raised the need to discuss the Christian duty to take the gospel to the nations, the older ministers practically scoffed at him. The very pastor who had baptized Carey coolly replied: "Young man, sit down. When God pleases to convert the heathen, he will do it without your aid or mine!"[20]

Thankfully, Carey saw clearly that the Great Commission applied to him in the 1790s, just as it applies to us today. He saw that not all of the nations had yet been reached in his day, just as they have not in ours. He also saw that at the end of Matthew 28:20, Jesus says, "Behold, I am with you always, to the end of the age." In other words, Jesus is with us to fulfill this commission until he returns.

Mission Exists Because Worship Doesn't

The message that runs through the Bible is the good news of God's own mission to fulfill his covenant promises through Jesus the Messiah. And the central mission of the Bible is to proclaim this message. But at the end of the day, this mission is not about us. It is not even about the people we are trying to reach. The mission is about the glory of God.

In his book *Let the Nations Be Glad*, John Piper writes: "Missions exists because worship doesn't. Worship is ultimate, not missions, because God is ultimate, not man."[21] At the beginning of this book, we saw how God is central to this story. His glory is central, not ours. If we think about the mission statement of the Bible, this is where it must begin and end. We are called to bring God glory. As more and more people turn to him in faith and repentance, his glory shines brighter and brighter. As we step into this story and join in his mission, we cannot forget it is *his* mission. And we get the privilege of being a part of it!

Connecting Verses

Old Testament: Isaiah 66:19
New Testament: Matthew 28:18–20

Summary Statement

To know the whole message of the Bible, we must know that from the beginning, God has been committed to the mission of bringing glory to himself through the salvation of his people.

WHERE TO GO NEXT

My prayer is that, as we've traced these sixteen words, you've been drawn into the drama of Scripture in a new way and are now motivated to continue the journey. If so, you might be wondering where to go next.

First, don't let this be a simple intellectual exercise. We have all sinned against the God who made us and are guilty before him. But his Son, Jesus, came to earth, lived a perfect life, and died the death we all deserve. He has risen from the dead and is now calling people from all over the world to follow him in repentance and faith. If you are studying the message of the Bible and have not submitted to the Lord of the Bible, then please turn from your sin and cast yourself on him.

If you want to know the message of the Bible, then you need to read the Bible. Try to read it all the way through once per year. Trace the connections between the Old Testament and the New Testament. See where you agree and disagree with the connections I'm making. As you read, apply and live out the mission of God in whatever places God might put you.

Finally, if you want to be a better biblical theologian—and you should—I think it is important to have a good grasp of the overall story of the Bible. If you need help there, my book *The*

Whole Story of the Bible in 16 Verses and the recommended resources I list at the end could be useful to you. Along with those books, I want to recommend three more resources to help you take a few more steps in your study of biblical theology:

- James M. Hamilton Jr., *What is Biblical Theology? A Guide to the Bible's Story, Symbolism, and Patterns* (Crossway, 2014), 127 pages. In this accessible introduction, Hamilton gets under the hood of biblical theology to give you some key tools to help advance your study.
- Edmund D. Clowney, *The Unfolding Mystery: Discovering Christ in the Old Testament* (P&R, 1988), 208 pages. One of the keys to understanding the whole message of the Bible is learning to read the Old Testament like the New Testament writers did: as a book about Jesus. I don't know of many better guides for this task than Clowney.
- T. Desmond Alexander, Brian S. Rosner, D. A. Carson, Graeme Goldsworthy, eds., *New Dictionary of Biblical Theology* (InterVarsity Press, 2000), 866 pages. This is more of a resource and tool than something you'll read straight through. But if you are serious about learning more about biblical theological themes throughout the Bible, this is a great book to have on your shelf.

NOTES

1. Jonathan D. Leavitt and Nicholas J. S. Christenfeld, "Story Spoilers Don't Spoil Stories," *Psychological Science* 20 (2011): 1–3.
2. J. R. R. Tolkien, *The Hobbit: or, There and Back Again* (Boston: Houghton Mifflin, 1937), 10.
3. For some examples, see Pss. 9:7; 22:3; 29:10; 33:14; 55:19; 80:1; 99:1; 102:12; 123:1.
4. Jonathan Edwards, *The Works of Jonathan Edwards* (Edinburgh: Banner of Truth, 1974), 1:102.
5. Anne Lamott, *Bird by Bird: Some Instructions on Writing and Life* (New York: Anchor Books, 1995), 55.
6. If you'd like to read more about this, look at Bruce Waltke with Cathi J. Fredricks, *Genesis: A Commentary* (Grand Rapids, MI: Zondervan, 2001), 128–29.
7. We all stand on the shoulders of those who have come before us, and I'm certainly no exception. In this chapter, I'm leaning on the work of two of my seminary professors, Peter Gentry and Stephen Wellum. For more on their understanding of covenants, check out their book *God's Kingdom through God's Covenants: A Concise Biblical Theology* (Wheaton, IL: Crossway, 2015). If you are up to a bigger challenge, check out their 848-page, not-so-concise book *Kingdom through Covenant: A Biblical-Theological Understanding of the Covenants* (Wheaton, IL: Crossway, 2012).
8. I'm unapologetically dependent on Peter Gentry and Stephen Wellum for helping me articulate the idea of "kingdom through covenant." See *God's Kingdom through God's Covenants: A Concise Biblical Theology* (Wheaton, IL: Crossway, 2015) or the longer *Kingdom through Covenant: A Biblical-Theological Understanding of the Covenants* (Wheaton, IL: Crossway, 2012).

9. Jeremy Treat, *The Crucified King: Atonement and Kingdom in Biblical and Systematic Theology* (Grand Rapids, MI: Zondervan, 2014), 247.

10. Ed Diener and Robert Biswas-Diener, *Happiness: Unlocking the Mysteries of Psychological Wealth* (Malden, MA: Blackwell, 2008), 53.

11. John R. W. Stott, *The Letter of John*, Tyndale New Testament Commentaries, vol. 19, rev. ed. (Grand Rapids, MI: Eerdmans, 1988), 199.

12. David Foster Wallace, *This is Water: Some Thoughts, Delivered on a Significant Occasion, about Living a Compassionate Life* (New York: Little, Brown, 2009), 99–101. Thanks to David Griffiths for this reference.

13. G. K. Beale, *We Become What We Worship: A Biblical Theology of Idolatry* (Downers Grove, IL: IVP, 2008), 16.

14. I owe most of the insights in this paragraph to Beale, *We Become What We Worship*, 202–20.

15. John Calvin, *Institutes of the Christian Religion*, ed. John T. McNeill, trans. Ford Lewis Battles, The Library of Christian Classics, vols. XX–XXI (Louisville: Westminster John Knox, 1960), 1.11.8.

16. C. S. Lewis, *Surprised by Joy: The Shape of My Early Life* (New York: Houghton Mifflin Harcourt, 1966), 207.

17. My thinking in this chapter, and especially the idea of "salvation through judgment," was influenced by James M. Hamilton Jr., *God's Glory in Salvation through Judgment: A Biblical Theology* (Wheaton, IL: Crossway, 2010).

18. See Brian S. Rosner, *Paul and the Law: Keeping the Commandments of God*, New Studies in Biblical Theology (Downers Grove, IL: InterVarsity Press, 2013), 135–206.

19. In response to the statement, "The Holy Spirit is a force, not a personal being," 31 percent agreed strongly and 32 percent agreed somewhat. Only 13 percent disagreed strongly, while 8 percent disagreed somewhat and 15 percent were not sure. Ligonier Ministries, "The State of Theology: Theological Awareness Benchmark Study," 28, http://ligonier-static-media.s3.amazonaws.com/uploads/thestateoftheology/TheStateOfTheology-FullSurveyKeyFindings.pdf, accessed January 7, 2016.

20. Quoted in Timothy George, *Amazing Grace: God's Pursuit, Our Response*, 2nd ed. (Wheaton, IL: Crossway, 2011), 107.

21. John Piper, *Let the Nations Be Glad: The Supremacy of God in Missions* (Grand Rapids, MI: Baker, 1993), 11.

GENERAL INDEX

SCRIPTURE INDEX

16 Verses.
1 Story.

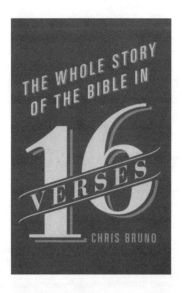

"Whether you're new to the Bible or have grown up hearing its stories in Sunday school, Bruno's book will lead you to a greater love for God's Word and hope in the Savior to whom every part of it points."

J. MACK STILES, CEO, Gulf Digital Solutions; General Secretary, Fellowship of Christian UAE Students (FOCUS), United Arab Emirates; author, *Evangelism*

"All Christians, whether mature or young in the faith, will find much to meditate on and rejoice in as Bruno faithfully sketches in the story of redemption."

THOMAS R. SCHREINER, James Buchanan Harrison Professor of New Testament Interpretation and Associate Dean of the School of Theology, The Southern Baptist Theological Seminary

For more information, visit crossway.org.